Praise for *The Media Ecosystem*

"Twenty-first-century media is a moving target. In *The Media Ecosystem*, Antonio López helps us understand the multi-faceted (and more importantly, multi-cultural) aspects of delivering critical information in today's world. Learn from nature and López's book, and carry on the good fight!"

— Randy Hayes, founder of Rainforest Action Network and director of Foundation Earth

"The turning point in López's *The Media Ecosystem* is the call for archetypal intelligence through his citation of parallels between ancient Hopi traditions and his own anti-colonial urban punk scene. López is one of his generation's original social thinkers. This book is urgent and chock-full of savage insights."

— Chellis Glendinning, author of *My Name Is Chellis and I'm in Recovery from Western Civilization*

"Antonio López has accomplished the Herculean task of creating a powerful manifesto for the media world! This is a thoughtful, challenging, and inspiring book, a wake-up call to all journalists, editors, writers, and publishers. The book is a plea for media men and women to help to create a sustainable, resilient, and joyful future in which people and nature can live in harmony with each other."

— ...ditor in chief of *Resurgence* magazine

"Combining media savvy, earth wisdom, and a deeply ethical account of today's attention politics, López hacks his way through the noosphere while keeping his feet on the ground. Sharp and accessible, *The Media Ecosystem* provides practical models for a green mediascape that will help us re-occupy the planet and the human imagination."

— Erik Davis, author of *Nomad Codes: Adventures in Modern Esoterica* and host of the radio show *Expanding Mind*

The Media Ecosystem

What Ecology Can Teach Us about Responsible Media Practice

Antonio López

Berkeley, California

Published by EVOLVER EDITIONS,
an imprint of North Atlantic Books
P.O. Box 12327
Berkeley, California 94712

Cover art by Nicola López: "Monument III" (2004);
Intaglio on paper; 10.75" x 8.5"
Art direction and cover design by michaelrobinsonnyc.com
Book design by Brad Greene

Printed in the United States of America

The Media Ecosystem: What Ecology Can Teach Us about Responsible Media Practice is sponsored by the Society for the Study of Native Arts and Sciences, a nonprofit educational corporation whose goals are to develop an educational and cross-cultural perspective linking various scientific, social, and artistic fields; to nurture a holistic view of arts, sciences, humanities, and healing; and to publish and distribute literature on the relationship of mind, body, and nature.

North Atlantic Books' publications are available through most bookstores. For further information, visit our Web site at www.northatlanticbooks.com or call 800-733-3000.

Library of Congress Cataloging-in-Publication Data

López, Antonio.
The media ecosystem : what ecology can teach us about responsible media practice / Antonio López.
p. cm.
ISBN 978-1-58394-459-2
1. Human ecology—Philosophy. 2. Green movement. I. Title.
GF21.L66 2012
304.201—dc23

2012006177

1 2 3 4 5 6 7 8 9 UNITED 17 16 15 14 13 12
Printed on 100 percent recycled paper

Contents

Pretext:
Reoccupying the Collective Imagination

Earth embodies a great spirit, of which we are all a part.

But alienated humans have colonized this planetary life force. Working in service of corporate abstractions, they have forsaken membership in the Earth community for the power and privilege to exploit all its resources and living subjects. Despite being children of Earth, they no longer know from where they come. Instead they enclose commonly shared resources, altering the chemistry of the atmosphere and oceans in order to transform our biosphere into a buyosphere. These ecological imperialists cannibalize the living systems they depend on. Not only do they subsist by eating the world, they colonize the media in order to harvest the system's most valuable resource: human consciousness.

The corporate project of savage capitalism is a colonial war on the spirit of Earth, *anima mundi,* the all-encompassing life force of minerals, water, air, plants, animals, and humans. Through creativity and the capacity to learn, anima mundi represents the self-regulating power of the world that guides evolution and life. It is both our ancient past . . . and our ancient future.

Rather than acting as a parasite on its life force, human culture should act as part of Earth's immune system. Such an immune system is encompassed by the cultural commons, the uncommodified activities and mutual support that are key to evolving our species. The cultural commons includes food recipes, agricultural knowledge, spiritual traditions, rituals, healing practices, language, everyday skills, crafts, songs, games, political conventions, and philosophical knowledge. In traditional land-based cultures, the vast array of practices that enables them to survive from year to year are passed between generations, sometimes refined and built upon, but always based on the condition that culture remain "all that we share."

Characteristics of the cultural commons include reciprocity, mutual support, participation, intergenerational dialogue, self-sufficiency, and receptiveness. Ultimately these practices and behaviors derive from knowledge gleaned from inhabiting the biggest commons of all: Earth. Therefore, the cultural commons is integral to sustainability and is the last line of defense against the fencing off and privatization of life on Earth. For a sustainable cultural commons to thrive, we need organic media that promotes green cultural citizenship and an Earth Democracy. Coined by Vandana Shiva, *Earth Democracy* represents the Indian concept of *vasudhaiva kutumbakam,* Earth family, which encompasses the planetary community of beings that comprise our living systems. Because corporate media and gadget companies promote technological "progress" while excluding living systems from our awareness, organic media practitioners are charged with the responsibility of incorporating an Earth perspective into their engagement of media ecosystems.

The French theologian Pierre Teilhard de Chardin

argued that if the biosphere is all that contains life on Earth, then a *noosphere* contains our collective consciousness. The semiotic version of a noosphere is the *semiosphere,* which is the totality of human signs and symbols. Anthropologist Wade Davis envisions an *ethnosphere,* which contains the totality of human cultural and linguistic diversity. The space of mediated civic engagement refers to the *public sphere.* The *mediasphere* is an all-encompassing media ecosystem that mixes these various concepts: a mediated cultural commons that facilitates planetary communications.

As a space of appearance that shapes our interconnected reality, the mediasphere can make visible the spirit of Earth. Imagine the healing and bridging potential of a healthy, conscientious, democratic media space. Unfortunately, the mediasphere is largely colonized by corporate forces that propagate an unsustainable model of unlimited growth and technological progress. This domination is represented by the increased monopolization of traditional mass media (TV, film, popular culture, news, etc.), the commercialization of the internet, and an unsustainable system of media gadget consumption. If unchecked, corporate media's power to shape our collective imagination inhibits our ability to envision alternatives beyond a colonial model of the world, in which a handful of megacorporations privatizes the planetary commons at the expense of the public good and living systems.

Resistance to corporate domination of the planet is reflected in the struggle for control of the mediasphere between the concentrated wealth holders of the planet and the global majority. Colonized media coordinates the interests of the corporate kleptocracy; decolonized media emerges from daily practice and the communication habits of people. The former is vertically structured and controlled by a handful of multinational megacorporations; the latter constitutes the horizontally networked communications environment that makes up the rest of the global mediasphere.

As such, we see hope in people's movements around the world: across the planet citizens take root, occupying the last remnants of the commons. Through self-mediation and network savvy, occupations glocalize their struggles by linking local conditions with a larger globalized network. In the process they engage in a kind of cultural citizenship that is shifting planetary culture toward an Earth Democracy. It's represented by systems theorist Ervin Laszlo's call to consciously evolve civilization from conquest, colonization, and consumerism to connection, communication, and consciousness. In short, through active engagement we can transition the cultural commons from "my space" to "our space."

Media's collective "myth space" is shifting from the top-down, transmission-based media of the Industrial Age to ritual communication. Ritual draws on the ancient traditions at the root of communication: commune, commonness, community, and communion. Through the occupation and reclamation of public spaces and the cultural commons—done in the spirit of conviviality, democracy, and connectivity—we can chart a new course of planetary evolution. When these physical spaces hybridize with global networks, they create an interconnected swarm of raised consciousness.

To this end, we can instigate a kind of media occupation that accelerates the emergent democratization of our collective imagination. *Occupy,* a transient verb, represents movement and transition in a number of ways: (1) seizing possession or control, (2) dwelling or residing in time or space, (3) residing as owner or tenant, (4) engaging attention, and (5) filling or performing a function. It should not be thought of as a noun or an end, but rather an action. Occupation doesn't mean taking over the TV studios or editorial offices of corporate media. It means staking a position as a node within a network that transcends the top-down propaganda machines of the past. Like the fluid media spaces we engage on a daily basis, sites of occupation are provisional, liminal zones. They politicize and socialize according to the form they take. These five dimensions are expressed by the following characteristics:

- *Seizing control.* The past five hundred years of colonization have resulted in the corporate occupation and theft of the global commons from Earth's human and nonhuman inhabitants. The consolidation of corporate control is leveraged by the monopolization of the symbolic order. Because media represent the planetary communications commons, such a space must remain open, transparent, diverse, and democratic. Occupying the media means reclaiming the cultural commons and envisioning alternate realities beyond the corporatocracy's vision of world enclosure.

- *Dwelling in time or space.* Colonization resulted in a disruption of our ancient sense of time and space, breaking our perceptual bonds with living systems. The antidote requires that we engage a participatory cosmology that reintegrates time and space into a shared reality that extends to global ecology. Our minds and bodies are designed to interact and engage with living systems. The rupture with and virtualization of living systems necessitates that we integrate our perception to acknowledge, respect, and engage the nonhuman world. Media should serve the purpose of making these connections more real and significant.

- *Residing.* We reside within embedded landscapes, from how we connect our senses with the environment to the bioregions that feed and nurture us. Occupying the media means the reinhabiting of not just public spaces but living systems. By hybridizing local issues with global movements, these actions glocalize the reclamation of the commons. Media occupation extends beyond the internet, cell phones, plazas, parks, and streets to how we inhabit the landscape of our lifeworld and within our own sense perception.

- *Engaging attention.* The colonizers' most precious commodity is our attention. Daily complacency and inattention enable the commodities system's ecocidal assault on the planet. Additionally, colonized media repackages and sells the time we spend doing things with media. Through media mindfulness we can allocate our energy through the careful application of our attention so that we no longer manufacture consciousness for the benefit of the corporatocracy.

- *Performing a function.* When one occupies a specific position within an organization (whether formal or informal), it entails a set of practices, skills, relationships, and expectations. It also means belonging to communities of practice with unspoken guidelines and norms. Whether working in traditional media companies and marketing firms, producing activist media, participating in education, or engaging in daily media practice, our global emergency calls for explicit ethics. Green cultural citizenship means articulating and thinking about the ethical orientation of our work, and engaging in mindful practice founded on a moral framework that puts the commons and the sacredness of life at the center of our attention.

Media occupation means applying green cultural citizenship to media ecosystems. Every media portal offers the chance for individuals to make the choice of whether to perpetuate the system of conquest and destruction or to become part of a greater evolution in which consciousness and connection build an Earth Democracy. Integral to this evolution is the reintegration of ecological intelligence into our daily practice, in particular how we use and make media. Media occupation and green cultural citizenship cannot be prescribed. There is no singular handbook or manual to direct its activities; the form of its practice comes through its doing and not through description or ideology. These particular practices emerge in the same way that dreaming merges creativity and learning to create new pathways of understanding.

The one thing we can be sure of is that the planet calls upon us to take action. Either we continue to reproduce the colonizers' planet-destroying delusions, or we restore the mediasphere's power balance by embracing the one advantage we have: our collective imagination. As such, we are too big to fail.

You are the ultimate mediator. As a medium of the planet's spirit, channel wisely.

CHAPTER 1

Green Cultural Citizenship

Scan any major news website for information about the environment and you will likely be led to two places: the science and weather sections. Even if there is an area solely devoted to environmental issues, in most cases the topic is treated as distinct from media, culture, or society (unless it impacts business, travel, or sports). This contrasts with an emerging view that sustainability, ecological awareness, and environmental consciousness need to be integrated and holistic. This mediasphere's particular landscape view, if you will, has its origins in the Western division of knowledge. In 1873 the German zoologist Ernst Haeckel coined the term *ecology,* basing it on the Greek word *oikos,* meaning "house, dwelling place, habitation." Likewise, *oikos* is also the root of *economics.* That ecology and economics were initially associated makes practical sense. As the great urbanist Jane Jacobs pointed out, both are intimately linked to the idea of household management. This concurs with the notion that sustainability is essentially how we approach the allocation of resources so as to not endanger future generations, but in a globalized world, the household must be conceived of on a planetary scale.

Households are primary sites of mediation. For example, the house is where we often work on the computer, watch TV, use our phones, share meals, and socialize, and all of these activities are mediated through language, metaphors, and economic practices. Economic globalization is intimately integrated into our homes through the goods we consume, the power we use, the food we eat, the waste we generate, and the culture we share.

If we look at household as a planetary concept (akin to Buckminster Fuller's Spaceship Earth), it is vastly more expansive than the meaning assigned to it by the Greeks, given that such a global worldview is facilitated by electronically disseminated media or air and space travel. Maps, images from space, books about travel to remote places, film, pictures in *National Geographic,* 24/7 news streams, and the internet are all aspects of how many of us picture and hold an image of Earth. This is not to say other cultures at different times in history did not have a holistic or comprehensive understanding of Earth. Indeed, home for many ancient cultures extended to the cosmos. But their perceptions were also grounded in their immediate surroundings, and their ability to survive depended on an intimate knowledge of the land they dwelled in (for what it's worth, many in the world still live this way today).

In many ways, then, mass media have facilitated "planetary" awareness, best symbolized by Marshall McLuhan's aphorism that we all now inhabit a global village. Though we know in practice that there is no such thing as a global village (the scales are contradictory), or that "global thinking" is problematic (we can't know how everyone thinks), the increasing view of our planetary interdependence and connectivity is clearly apparent and necessary. After all, no matter who pollutes the atmosphere, we all breathe the same air. The melting of glaciers in the Himalayas is not a disconnected event; it has a cascading impact on water supplies, food, migration, economy, and regional conflict that reverberates globally. Additionally, events like the Icelandic volcano ash cloud, Indian Ocean tsunami, or the Haitian earthquake highlight the global character of calamity. The impact on global weather by the proverbial butterfly's wing flapping in Brazil should be less an abstract mental exercise in chaos theory and more of a graspable metaphor for the daily interconnected lives of all of us.

Awareness of global issues, whether we like it or not, is mostly mediated. Such networked mediation should enable us to grasp the matrix connecting a locally grounded reality with its international strands, such as when we buy food (choosing when possible whether it is local, fair trade, or biological/organic). We can also analyze the production stream of our shoes and other consumer goods, connecting them with the culture industry and globalized production stream in order to build a heightened awareness of the interconnected lives between consumers, workers, and the nonhuman world. Finally, the very electronic equipment we use has global implications in terms of energy consumption, mineral extraction for precious metals, water usage for chip manufacturing, and the massive trade in toxic waste that results from the built-in obsolescence of our "cheap" electronics ("cheap" because we don't factor in the external costs that are borne by unequal labor conditions and the material cost of the environment).

Consequently, one of the primary sites of contact with the larger global system is through media. Globalization, consumerism, industrialization, and information economy are accelerating the ecological crisis, and media helps facilitate this process by masking its dangers and touting the benefits of this system through the uncontested worship of growth, technology, progress, and consumerism. Critically engaging media—whether it's advertising, news, or popular culture—provides opportunities to connect our daily perception with the bigger picture (a media metaphor!).

As modern subjects we occupy a hybridized conceptual space that blends firsthand and mediated experiences. Our lifeworld is simultaneously "here" and "there." The trouble is finding the right terminology to describe the reality of our multidimensional experience that eschews the normal dichotomy between natural and unnatural, real and simulated, or organic versus synthetic. Our experience is simultaneously natural, electronically mediated, interdependent, and global.

Meanwhile, the nonhuman world is in communication with us in every moment through multiple channels. We are always negotiating this communication in some way, albeit mostly unconsciously. There are multiple cues from the environment telling us that our living systems are sick and weakened by our behavior, whether they be mass die-offs from birds, beached mammals, collapsing bee colonies, or crazy weather. The arts of reading snowdrifts, wave swells, cloud formations, dune formations, and plant pollination are just some of the various skills that could help us communicate better with living systems. Unfortunately, most of us either ignore these signs or have diminished sense perception.

One way to reconcile this is to borrow from the school of socioenvironmental thought that looks at integrating our concepts of "world system" and "Earth system." From this perspective, economics and ecology recursively impact each other. For example, researchers found an important correlation between the Sony PlayStation 2 and the decline of the gorilla population in the Democratic Republic of Congo. In 2000 speculation on the price of tantalum, a key precious metal used in microelectronics such as cell phones and gaming devices, was driven by the impending release of the PlayStation 2. This led to a massive mining boom in the Congo's Kahuzi-Biega national park, severely impacting the population of many animal species, including elephants, tortoises, birds, and small mammals. The park is home of the Grauer's gorilla, which represents 86 percent of the planetary population of lowland gorillas. As a result of the tantalum rush, the Grauer's gorilla population declined from seventeen thousand to three thousand. Fueled by consumer demand for gadgets and market speculation driven by internet trading, this tragedy reflects the problem of an economic paradigm that fails to account for living systems. The inability of media and gadget companies to incorporate an Earth system ethic into their design leads to a loss of biodiversity. Not only is it immoral to create systems that disregard life, such a loss has huge implications for the climate, for as we decrease biodiversity, regional ecosystems lose the ability to thrive and adjust under conditions of the extreme ecological disruptions that are increasingly commonplace.

Climate change is the single most important issue of our lifetime, which cannot be addressed except from a thoroughly holistic perspective. In this sense, we need a wide-angle view to bring the larger awareness of global ecological and social systems into the discussion of media (without it being "ghettoized" by the specific polemics of environmentalism or globalization). It is my contention that relegating issues of ecology and globalization to their normal professional and thought divisions means missing an opportunity to confront the problem where we come into contact with it on a daily basis—through our communication systems—and denying that they are intimately linked.

Viewing media outside the context of sustainability is part of the problem. The relationship between them is twofold: ecological footprint (material impact) and mindprint (mental impact). Material issues include the toxins used to make gadgets and their impact on the health of workers and their communities; the CO_2 emissions of fossil fuels needed to run our electronic networks (which is now equal to the global aviation industry); and the e-waste generated from overconsumption. The ecological mindprint of media includes their impact on our perception of time, space, and our sense of "place"; the enabling of a destructive globalized growth economy via a symbolic architecture of brands, stocks, and money; the perpetuation of consumerism through marketing; the spread of disinformation and propaganda that hinders efforts to mitigate the effects of climate change; and the maintenance of a destructive symbolic order through culture-industry products like TV programming, music videos, film, and video games. While it's true that social media and the internet enable us to "amplify our minds" (as Howard Rheingold suggests) or accumulate "cognitive surplus" (as Clay Shirky argues), unless we reintegrate a sense of ecological well-being into our media practice, we will not be able to enjoy the benefits of technology that we celebrate. To put it in stark terms, when it comes to the internet, the imagination is limitless, but when it comes to living systems we have to obey the laws of nature. Civilization and all its wonderful media gadgets will not thrive or exist if the current treatment of our living systems does not change.

Ecological Intelligence

As Einstein famously said, we cannot solve problems with the same kind of thinking that created them. The shift to an ecologically oriented media requires that we look at our mental model of the world. The root of the problem is that we privilege mechanism over ecological intelligence. Mechanism is a machine metaphor for nature and forms the primary knowledge paradigm of the Industrial-Scientific Revolution. It is expressed by the beliefs that minds are programmed by symbolic representations (i.e., a mind is a machine with language as its software) and that humans are disconnected, autonomous beings independent from their living habitats. In terms of media, the logic of mechanism leads to the "thingification" of information and communication.

Ecological intelligence is based on the concept that people are part of "thinking systems" that extend beyond their bodies into the spaces they embody. The internet gives us a good model for visualizing this: since we define ourselves based on the cues of our environment, the feedback system of our extended mind on the net constantly impacts our self-definition. The way that we connect and share ourselves with others on the net influences our behavior and understanding of who we are. Because of our mirror neurons, we have the capacity for empathy, or what Daniel Goleman calls emotional intelligence. In a book he co-authored, *Primal Leadership,* Goleman argues that the limbic system has an open loop emotional center that depends on connecting with other people to stabilize our emotions. If this is true on the internet, why not forests and deserts? Didn't our ancient ancestors similarly define themselves via their environments, since communication with animals and living systems was necessary for survival?

Ecopsychologists, who argue that our disconnection with nature actually makes us psychotic, would concur with Goleman but extend his reasoning to our need and capacity to connect with animals and living systems. Ecopsychologists argue that when we abandoned our "ontogenesis" with nature—a coming into being through bonding with the world spirit—we took a turn from sustainable Neolithic cultures that thrived for thousands of years to ones dominated by murdering and misogyny. We no longer have coming of age rituals that enable us to enter into a deep union with our inhabited landscape.

Traces of our ancient past can be found in how children are allowed to play as if animals, plants, or spirits can talk to them. But by confining these behaviors to childhood, we treat our ancient selves as just childish versions of our adult, modern identities. This is best exemplified by animations targeting children. Often these neonatal representations that depict cartoon animals with big heads to resemble toddlers reinforce a hierarchy of relations in which animals are represented as undeveloped humans. Furthermore, Disney's cultural monopolization of "magic" demonstrates just how far we have transitioned from living systems to a technocratic environment where our primal connection with Earth is infantilized by Disney imagineers. Contrast this with the work of Japanese animator Hayao Miyazaki, whose respectful tales of nature spirits in films like *My Neighbor Totoro, Spirited Away,* and *Princess Mononoke* serve as ecological allegories of connection. Or *FernGully*'s effort to tackle deforestation. While it's true that Disney did serve up a powerful salvo against the consumer culture with *Wall-E,* one has to wonder if

Disney's business model of mass merchandizing and outsourced production walks the talk.

Communications theorist James Carey argues that we have a public self—that is, it is socially constructed and cannot exist without mutually shared reality. For example, our thoughts are shaped through language and feedback from our social networks. His error—as is the case of most communication theory—is that the environment is absent from this context. In fact, one of the greatest problems and challenges is the symbolic annihilation of the environment from practically any discussion of social theory. Gregory Bateson was one of the few who could see beyond this problem. Bateson argues that each of us is an "organism plus environment." Consider the simple fact that we can't live without breathing air, drinking water, or eating food. We are composed of and depend upon the environment. As Bateson says so succinctly, if you destroy the environment, you destroy the organism. Never mind the technological fantasy of the singularity, in which we can upload our consciousness into computers. It will never happen because our consciousness cannot be separated from living systems: they coevolve, coexist, and are codependent. Even computers depend on natural systems and resources to exist. The singularity is a badly conceived waste of human intelligence and probably the best example of mechanistic thinking gone haywire.

The example of Disney's *Wall-E* exemplifies how less unsustainable media practice doesn't necessarily lead to sustainable cultural production. Thus, we should guard against approaches to ecological intelligence that are solely aimed at lessening the impact of mechanistic economic practices. For example, Goleman failed to apply his own concept of open loop emotional intelligence when he penned *Ecological Intelligence.* Here, Goleman argues that if products were made more transparent, people would change their buying habits and therefore make the system more sustainable. An example of this would be a smartphone app that can scan a product's barcode and give consumers transparent information about its supply chain. Apps tailored toward green consumption could enable buyers to determine which products meet the highest ecological standards. While this kind of transparency is a step in the right direction, it also assumes that changing an unsustainable paradigm is a matter of changing information. In other words, all we need to do is reprogram our mental software to become sustainable.

Unfortunately, buying sustainable TVs (an oxymoron) will not lead to a deep breakthrough in how we as a culture relate to the world. Goleman's "ecological intelligence" is a technological solution to a spiritual/worldview problem, one that needs to be addressed through reconceptualizing the autonomous self. Changing consumer information as an environmental solution is putting the cart before the donkey. Goleman's approach is more like an ecological version of the CIA than a change in how we perceive the world. Furthermore, his glee for monitoring consumer habits through brain scans is too weird to even consider viable. It takes the technological solution too far, reducing the notion of ecological intelligence to a matter of brainwave patterns, and not one of an embodied connection to the world. I'm not deriding the concept of transparent business practices—it is in fact one of the best by-products of networked media. I just object to the idea that intelligence can simply be "upgraded" as if it were an operating system made by Microsoft.

An expanded concept of the self would not only be part of a larger system (as opposed to competing with it), it would revitalize the important emotional qualities that products are marketed to replace. Advertising often appeals to a desire for authenticity and community, but rarely delivers. It's the emotional equivalent of eating empty-calorie food produced by industrial food corporations. The well-intended appeal for transparent corporate practices is based on the essential urges described by ecopsychologists—it comes down to a desire for connection, which is part of our inherent evolutionary need to bond with nature.

A society based on a mechanistic worldview is inherently exploitative: it treats the world as a collection of objects. You can trace a straight line from this mode of perception to enclosure, colonialism, uninhibited growth of corporations, and media monopoly. Mechanism is tied to exploitation because when the world is composed of things, living systems are reduced to disconnected resources that exist for the purpose of human use—or inhuman, as is the case of corporate entities taking over the cultural commons and planetary living systems.

Lessons from the First Occupation

The systematic destruction and globalized marginalization of ecological intelligence is expressed more clearly by the process of colonization. We can start by looking at how this unfolded during the European conquest of the Americas. When Hernán Cortés invaded Mexico, he said it was because he was afflicted with a disease, and that gold was the only cure. For the past five hundred years this disease has spread around the world and afflicted many cultures. The Australian Nunga call it the Invader Dreaming: the dominator complex or collective psychosis that drives conquest and colonial parasitism in the name of "progress." The Nunga, who have lived on the Australian continent anywhere from 40,000 to 125,000 years, believe groups have their own particular belief systems—"dreamtime"—be they ants, sharks, or European settlers. To them the Invader Dreaming is a weapon of mass cultural destruction.

The conditions of North America's European occupations were a violent disruption of time and space that few of us can comprehend. The consequence of this historical condition—modernity—is an upside-down world in which this disturbance is normal. But when Native Americans—or First Nations—first contacted the Spanish, the European way of being in the world was alien to them. Just as we view Earth-invading aliens in sci-fi movies as disastrous and strange, to the original inhabitants of the Americas European colonists were incomprehensible monsters.

One of the most ancient cultures of North America is that of the Hopi, who have occupied their lands in what is modern-day Arizona for thousands of years. They first came into contact with the Spanish in 1540. Back when the Hopi initially gathered to discuss the Castilians' intentions and how to deal with them, they looked closely at the Spaniard's dominant symbol, the crucifix, and interpreted it as a sign of great engineering skills and angular thinking. From this symbol, they understood the Spanish to be masters of the material and mental realm. But they were concerned about one thing, and it was a big worry. Where was the circle? The medicine wheel, a common emblem of North American First Nations, comprises an encircled cross. It represents an integral system that maps the cosmos from the macro to the micro levels, a kind of mandala for psychological and spiritual orientation. With both linear and holistic elements, the cross and circle together represent the four directions and the continuity of life. It's also the modern astronomical symbol for Earth.

As a symbol, a cross alone lacks holism. To the Hopi, this meant that the Spanish were very dangerous people. Indeed, at the time of the conquest of the Americas, Spanish invaders were at the cusp of the Industrial-Scientific Revolution, pushing the boundaries of European subjectivity by embracing a Cartesian sense of space, a kind of perception that maps, plots, and reigns in three-dimensional grids. They could "rule" at a distance through the technology of writing, which bureaucratized colonization and instituted hierarchical systems of control. Against weapons, logistics, and disease, the First Nations of the Americas had little chance of defending themselves. Despite the violent revolt against Spanish rule in what is now the southwestern United States, little could stop the impending invasion of American-style capitalism and its insidious tools of control: education and media.

The Hopi's insight into the European's invader mentality derived not just from direct experience with the consequences of the system imposed upon them, but also from their ancient ritual practices and connection with the land, which enabled them to defamiliarize themselves with the Spaniard's prevailing symbol and its attendant ideology (ideology being the totality of taken-for-granted assumptions about how the world works). Now, with the Hopi's air poisoned and springs dried in order to power casinos in Las Vegas and sports stadiums in Phoenix, it's imperative that the rest of us understand intimately the machinations behind the destruction of ecosystems and those cultures that evolved within them.

The Hopi's initial deconstruction of the crucifix came from their outsider perspective. The lesson for us modern folks is for us to see our symbolic reality with fresh eyes. We must make our world strange in order to see it anew. One way to do this is to borrow from bioregional activists who locate their work within specific ecosystems. Peter Berg, a leading activist of contemporary bioregional philosophy, says that a bioregion is "a geographic terrain and a terrain of consciousness." To land-based cultures—or biocultures—like the Hopi, land and culture are part of the commons, because both are shared by everyone. In their pursuit of remote control and extraction of other people's resources, colonialists survive by destroying the commons and those cultures that evolved within specific landscapes.

The goal of colonization, and its key implication for media, is that people have to be trained to take on an alien perspective as their own. In one example, the great anticolonial writer Frantz Fanon described this psychological condition as having black skin with a white mask. We adapt the mentality and belief systems of colonization as a mask, with media encouraging us to accept exploitation as normal and even desirable. We may not call the modern system of savage capitalism and primitive accumulation of resources colonization, but the very practice of contemporary economics is in all but name the takeover and extraction of the wealth of Earth and its majority inhabitants. The increasing disparity between the so-called 1 percent of wealth holders and the other 99 percent reflects how colonization has extended to average middle-class people. Few are immune to its effects, and corporate media do their bit to ensure that we accept this absurdity as normal. Not only do they encourage us to take on the mask of colonizer, it makes it so normal that it becomes invisible.

In terms of the media's ecological mindprint, an important lesson from the Hopi encounter with the Spanish is the indigenous insight (as in being of a particular land-based tradition) of the importance of symbolic environments. Symbols act like sigils, which are used by alchemists to access knowledge and magic. In the case of the cross, one of its most potent powers is to define what is and isn't sacred. If the altar inside the church is the access point to the sacred, then everything else is not. Isolating and narrowing the space of the revered to a confined, controlled, and human-constructed hierarchy of divinity facilitates the exploitation of the Other. If you are not sanctioned by this tightly controlled system, then you might as well go to hell.

Our gadgets act as magical devices with symbols that give us access to certain kinds of knowledge, such as corporate brands, stock quotes, and entertainment. By contrast, the Native American medicine wheel offers an alternative model for understanding the world and holistically integrating our communications and technologies into a more sustainable vision for the future.

Bridging the Ancient Future

I learned the story of the circle and cross from Thomas Banyacya, an elder of the Hopi, whom I had the privilege of staying with when I was fifteen as part of a high school program. In 1992, ten years after my stay, Thomas accompanied a group of Hopi spokespeople to warn the UN's General Assembly about the consequences of perpetuating business as usual. In his presentation to the General Assembly, Thomas described the meaning of an ancient inscription etched into a rock on Hopi lands that depicts two distinct directions for the future of humanity:

> *This rock drawing shows part of the Hopi prophecy. There are two paths. The first, with high technology but separate*

> *from natural and spiritual law, leads to these jagged lines representing chaos. The lower path is one that remains in harmony with natural law. Here we see a line that represents a choice like a bridge joining the paths. If we return to spiritual harmony and live from our hearts we can experience a paradise in this world. If we continue only on this upper path, we will come to destruction. . . . It's up to all of us, as children of Mother Earth, to clean up this mess before it's too late.*

To young people such as myself, Thomas liked to tell the story in more mythopoetic terms, about a time when white people and the Hopi were brothers that canoed together in the same river—until a certain point where their journeys forked. Though whites followed a particularly dangerous path far from their roots, they would someday rejoin and continue down the river as before, alongside the Hopi. Given how the Hopi have suffered over the years at the hands of Euro-American civilization, this is a rather hopeful story that belays the more apocalyptic vision presented to the UN. But it also shows their willingness to see people not for their skin color, but for what is in their hearts.

Banayacya warned of the danger that civilization without a proper moral compass will transform the biosphere into a buyosphere. This is achieved through a mindless embrace of communication technologies that are designed exclusively for consumerism. Technological progress, the Hopi warn, becomes a tautology, or self-justification. In the form of corporate media, these attitudes and beliefs synthesize into an all-pervasive ideology. As media consumers and producers we depend on gadgets to communicate and connect. As tools to think and connect with, they should also be instruments that serve living systems. If we use technology without heart, we begin to think and act like machines. We become gadgets for what the sociologist Immanuel Wallerstein calls the "world system"—a networked form of capitalism that increasingly pervades and cannibalizes the regional cultures of the globe. Under such conditions, we praise clever design interfaces and media content without regard to their impact on the workers or the health of living systems. Media designed for such a system then become disconnected from humanity's interdependence with living systems and ultimately serve one purpose: corporate colonialism of the cultural commons.

The Spanish cross has long since been replaced by the world system's master tropes: "technology," "progress," "growth," "freedom," and "democracy." These concepts permeate the mediasphere via visual and rhetorical referents, embedding our lifeworld so that we can no longer remember how the land or animals speak to us. The kind of world these symbols include and exclude should be of grave concern to anyone concerned with the health and well-being of global ecology. Thus, as we move forward in our efforts to bridge our ancient heritage with our future potential, we'll need to hack these systems to make them more friendly and amenable to the rhythms of nature and the immediate needs of the cultural commons.

Spirit of Earth

Now, let's do a gut check. When you hear or read *Gaia,* how does it feel in your body? When you see the photo of Earth from outer space, what emotions does it generate? If there is any feeling remotely like the sensation of beauty, compassion, empathy, or love, then your soul has not been completely devoured by the world system.

Unlike the alien-like mentality that permeates the world system, as earthlings we have an innate ability to empathize, feel love, experience beauty, seek connection, and desire wholeness. Our capacity for war, greed, destruction, and delusion is not unnatural, but neither is it normal or inevitable. It is the result of conditioning, manipulation, and trauma. The world according to this mentality is a scary and dangerous place, as evidenced by any random sample of the evening news. Rarely are we reminded that murder and terrorism are actually rare occurrences. Most of us have internal restraints against committing acts of violence. After all, mobilizing people for war requires more than a simple command. Even in battle, as was documented during WWII, many soldiers shoot to miss.

Ancient cultures, and in particular in the European tradition, believed in the anima mundi—world spirit. It is common for indigenous cultures to view the universe and all its creations as alive. So instead of the modern Euro-American cultural assumption, "I think, therefore I am," they believe, "It all thinks, therefore I am." They live in a participatory and reciprocal cosmos as opposed to a vertically controlled, hierarchically structured system of reality.

For many brought up with a scientifically oriented view of the world, this requires a conceptual leap. But if you can, try to suspend disbelief and play with the idea that because we as humans are of the world, we are connected to the planetary spirit that lives in everything, as was symbolized by the Na'vi in the film *Avatar.* Recall how the Na'vi could connect to a kind of planetary internet that allowed them to communicate with animals and plant spirits. This is not just sci-fi fantasy but a glimpse of our ancient past and the present reality of many peoples on Earth.

Such an awareness is actually dangerous to the status quo. It means great responsibility, because a cultural environment where everything is shared implies reciprocity. Not surprisingly, in the Buddhist tradition one of the first skills to be cultivated in contemplative practice is generosity. The act of volunteering and gifting helps us acknowledge that there is no boundary between people when connected through the heart. Give twenty dollars to someone you never met before and see what happens. It is quite magical.

Now, as it turns out, in 1997 ecological economists did the math and estimated that annually Earth "gives" us over $33 trillion of "free" services that we never pay for, which at the time of the study was about twice the gross national product of the world's economies. The spirit of generosity that is part of many traditional spiritual practices serves as restraint against wanton exploitation of our living systems. Many Native Americans, for example, set aside a small portion of every meal for their ancestors. This kind of practice instills a mindfulness that helps us remember that every meal is a gift and food shouldn't be taken for granted. We have to give back and not just take from the Earth whatever pleases us.

We take for granted the generosity that actually holds our whole system together. The official economy would not survive without the contributions of nature, homemakers, government expenditure, and social economy. We don't charge people to hold the door open or carry the groceries up the stairs. We don't ask to be compensated for recipes or learning the alphabet. Cooking, growing food, acquiring languages, literacy, and a host of day-to-day practices exist within a cultural commons that is directly responsible for the evolution and maintenance of human culture.

That sharing actually comes "naturally" to us indicates that at some point in our ancient history it was a necessary part of our evolutionary survival strategy as a response to the environment. Could it be that we actually learned reciprocity because it is a natural aspect of living systems in which cooperation and adaptation, rather than competition, are really the norm? Let's suppose this generosity of spirit, then, is intrinsic to who we are, and therefore it makes perfect sense that such behaviors are actually quite common in the realm of online media practice. Consider that the emergence of open source, Creative Commons, shareware, and open access are actually a built-in response to the cartelized media environment, and that "nature" actually abhors monopoly. (Keep in mind that corporations that drive monopolization are not "people" or "natural," despite their legal and ideological status under world system dominion.)

As the history of media and technological evolution has shown time and time again, early human uses of communication tools tend toward open systems, but once economic interests figure out how to fence off "freeloaders," these systems close down. Thus as we move from printing presses, telegraphs, radios, TV, and film to the internet, we seesaw between the free spirited, anarchic appropriation of communication tools to their closure and privatization. All too often the world system strikes again. But we can be heartened with the knowledge that communication—the ability to speak and be heard—is a fundamental right and an integral aspect of human evolution and learning. An ethical framework based on open systems in both personal practice and social policy is actually an expression of anima mundi, the world spirit.

To reiterate, colonialism is predicated on closed systems and hierarchical control. It extracts and accumulates resources from the commons and privatizes them. Closed systems lack participation and democracy. Open systems invite participation and citizenship. The former requires that people act like consumers, while the latter means engaged cultural citizenship.

Consumerism versus Green Citizenship

In 1934 Walter Benjamin outlined the concept of "author as producer," an argument that cultural producers such as professional writers are also cultural workers and should be conscious of whether or not they engage their crafts as part of a larger project of criticism and political activism. "Cultural work" was primarily seen as a politically progressive activity and distinguished from the kinds of production for profit that media monopolies engaged in. Similarly, the Italian Marxist Antonio Gramsci developed the idea of the "organic intellectual." He argued that all humans were intellectuals, but not all were granted the role of intellectual by the dominant society. As such, the governing economic class produces native intellectuals who tend to reproduce the interests of its class. He theorized that working-class intellectuals would play a revolutionary role.

During the era dominated by one-to-many mass media (roughly 1880–1990) it was easier to distinguish between the producers and consumers of information, and also between the "good guys" and "bad guys" of media production. During that time, as new media technologies emerged (such as telephony, film, radio, and television), the openness of media systems quickly gave way to closed media monopolies. Predominantly there were relatively small groups of media companies producing the majority of media content, which was distributed in a linear (top-down) fashion with very few feedback mechanisms. The concept of "independent" and "critical" media was clearer and easier to distinguish because marketing and corporate media had yet to incorporate the aesthetics, practices, and politics of alternative media into their offerings.

With the advent of postmodern media and the internet, these boundaries have become less clear. Corporate monopolies are now much larger, but aesthetically they have incorporated avant-garde aesthetics and the language of irony so as to co-opt the traditional tools of critical media. This includes the appropriation of environmentalism and sustainability rhetoric, which enables media makers to "greenwash" their organizations and practices. Such a climate makes "cultural work" more confusing.

Nonetheless, like the early days of telephony, radio, and film, with the rise of the internet, media's distribution and feedback structure has changed so that many more people can actively participate in the creation of media. Currently there is a rise in participatory culture, which is defined as a set of practices that includes easy access for creative expression and political engagement, a desire to share and connect with others, informal learning in which people freely share "how to" knowledge, and an atmosphere in which people care about what they do and care about what others think about them.

Participatory culture represents an extremely positive development in the evolution of media democracy, but it also needs to be problematized when its tools are also instruments of profit for large media platforms like Google and Facebook. Some critics argue that with the internet, we commodify our consciousness for the private companies that own the internet platforms we use. Again, this complicates the notion of "cultural work," since the spaces that a lot of political activism and civic engagement take place in are often privatized. How would this scheme fit in terms of Benjamin's concept of author as producer or Gramsci's idea of the organic intellectual?

A media practitioner is both a cultural worker and an organic intellectual of the contemporary media environment, whose role in new media's political economy is negotiated and ambiguous. Everything we do with new media involves a practice of some sort (whether conscious or not) and cultural production, whether we are reproducing the status quo, creating new culture, or a mix of the two. When we engage participatory media tools, we are products as much as producers of media. Additionally, with participatory media we also engage various communities of practice, be they LISTSERVS, online forums, or discussion groups.

But in terms of sustainability, does the average media practitioner relate daily activities of media engagement with his or her impact on living habitats? One way unsustainable cultural patterns repeat themselves is from a lack of consciousness of how our personal practices are connected to our living habitats. Consequently, inattentiveness and lack of awareness are why media users probably don't engage in sustainable cultural practices.

A media user who engages in sustainable cultural practices is an organic media practitioner. The behaviors of such a practitioner are ecologically intelligent responses to media practice that include the ability to reconnect an awareness of one's media usage with its physiological impact on the environment; to recognize media's phenomenological influence on one's perception of time, space, and place; to understand media's interdependence with the global economy; to be conscious of media's interaction with one's cultural beliefs; and to develop an ethical framework in order to act upon these understandings and to make wise choices.

The Ancient Future of Organic Media Practice

During my winter stay in Hopi in 1982, as part of the annual ritual cycle of their complex ceremonial structure, I encountered a coming-of-age ritual that involved the so-called "whipping" kachina, Angwusnasomtaka, Crow Mother. In Hopi ceremonial life kachinas are nature spirits that reside in the nearby San Francisco Peaks. During their ceremonies Hopi transform themselves into kachinas to perform various religious functions. The Angwusnasomtaka, donning a woven kilt and wooden mask with fists full of yucca, chases and whips kids who behaved badly during the previous year. The Angwusnasomtaka also likes to torment tourists. I, too, was hounded and terrified by this entity. At the time, being a young punk rocker from Los Angeles, the whole thing seemed very alien to me. Yet, to Hopi traditionalists, I was probably equally strange.

During one crisp winter night filled with galactic explosions of starry light and sweet cedar smoke, I entered into the earthen chamber of the kiva to encounter one of many all-night ceremonies taking place. Here different clans perform specific dances, so for the ceremonial cycle to be complete, every clan must participate. The kiva's underground circular design is a direct umbilical cord to the ancient spiritual practices of the Americas.

That night I witnessed wave after wave of kachina dancers entering and exiting the ceremonial womb via a hand-built ladder, shuffling on the dirt floor to steady drumbeats pounded by men with bandanas tied around their heads in a sidewise bun. During the all-night hypnotic blur of the dances, I began cross editing the circular motions and repetitive beats of the kiva with my own experiences at punk gigs. Slam dancing had a similar circular quality, and our furious punk riffs had a parallel monotony of the pounding drums that were now pulsating steadily like a heartbeat. What mattered was not so much the simplicity of the form but the participatory and organic character of the experience. Just as the Hopi in the kiva passed around colored popcorn as acts of reciprocity, in punk we, too, shared our wares and culture to those who joined.

Punks inadvertently repurposed the ancient traditions at the core of communication by embracing the spirit of commune, commonness, community, and communion. We were part of a lineage of Western cultural rebels that tapped into ancient human traditions. Seeing the parallel gave me an insight to the resilience and desire for authenticity within my own cultural realm. Despite living in a car-dependent, shopping-mall-paved landscape, punks were anti-colonists. We didn't want corporate culture, militarized politics, and Ronald Reagan's ilk dictating our reality. We were just teen skaters who knew nothing about the world except from our direct experience of living within it and its mediation through mass media. Yet there was something within us that pulled us toward creating an organic, authentic community. Rather than elements from the natural world, our subcultural reality was built with media and technology. Whether it was unconventional fashion, experimental art, guitar amplification, or photocopied zines and flyers, we had a simple philosophy: DIY, or "do it yourself." Becoming "more than a witness" was our means for channeling the spirit of our age. In our cut-up collages we didn't have corn or cloud motifs like the Hopi, but we did have the material of our lived reality to repurpose in order to create something participatory and real. We reoccupied our lifeworld, staking a position in opposition to corporate overlords.

Just as importantly, punk offered a bridge for diverse cultural groups that didn't have an outlet for creative expression in mainstream society. In the United Kingdom, working-class white youths and black immigrants found commonalities, best exemplified by the hybridization between punk and reggae heard in the music of bands like The Clash. In Washington, DC, the African American hardcore group Bad Brains interspersed reggae with a tornado of guitar riffs. As I experienced it in California, punk was a multicultural refuge for weirdos and rebels from a variety of backgrounds. It was one of the few places where the disenfranchised—such as Latinos, Asians, African Americans, gays, and women—had a safe space in which such distinctions didn't matter. Unfortunately, after punk became more widely represented and interpreted by sensationalistic mass media, bigots, racists, and jocks invaded the scene by donning punk fashion, but not its liberatory attitude. Subsequently many punks migrated into hip hop, as was the case with numerous Chicanos who embraced hip hop's broader multicultural expression of art and culture. Many Chicanos nurtured in the anarchist punk movement, like the members of the band Aztlan Underground, incorporated hip hop's call to connect with cultural origins by embracing their indigenous heritage and using their music and art as a platform for rooting their modern identities within the soil of their ancestral being. Thus, their cultural revival becomes a kind of educational mediation.

Indeed, more than any subculture, hip hop has been adapted by oppressed groups around the world as a means of reconnecting with their ancient traditions, revitalizing that which had been eroded by the various diasporas resulting from global migration, while at the same time tapping into a planetary youth culture of rebellion. As such, hip hop in its more grassroots, noncommercial variety represents a kind of organic media practice. In particular it revitalizes the spirit of ritual, communion, and community. As the artist Mike (360) Ipiotis highlights, hip hop has five dimensions of expression that, when working fluidly together, form the basis for holistic alternative cultural practice. For example, the hip hop community is composed of four major elements: writers (graffiti artists), DJs (turntabalists), B Boys and B Girls (break dancers), and MCs (rappers/poets). Equally vital but not always recognizable is the fifth element, the element of "building" (raising consciousness). In hip hop all these components work together cohesively, like when someone wants to throw a "jam" or party. The graf artist makes the flyer, the DJ provides the beats, the MC creates the context and narration, and B Boys rock the house.

Instead of being a subculture, Ipiotis considers hip hop a surrogate culture. Be it punk or hip hop, belonging to a vital movement is in essence being part of a tribe. For global youth whose traditions and cultures become marginalized, hip hop becomes a school of life. Literary and linguistic skills are taught through rapping; visual art and geometry skills are learned through graf art; mathematics and computer skills are learned through the musical forms (DJing and beat production); and break dancing is a de facto form of conditioning that can be likened to kung fu or the Brazilian capoeira, which combines martial arts and dance developed be West African slaves. Break dance's "up rock" can even resemble Native American fancy dancing or salsa.

DJs, also called turntabalists, are master technicians. Though it has been said that jazz was the African appropriation of European instruments, it can also be argued that hip hop is the reappropriation of Japanese technology for the art of awakening universal truths within us. Producers and mixers master the computers and audio technology, skills invaluable in a world that is increasingly divided by the information haves and have-nots. Yet hip hop is not technologically dependent. For example, in the absence of turntables or drum machines, one can accompany the freestyle or improvised poetry of rappers with beat boxing (vocalized percussion). As an oral culture hop hip disseminates information just as Spanish troubadours of old did when they sang of current events in plazas, or like West African griots who told old stories and spread news through song and music, or like the Puerto Rican plena drummers whose *periodico cantado* (sung newspaper) informed the illiterate poor of regional events and news.

To hard-core members of the hip hop community, each of the four components is to be mastered, while the fifth element of building consciousness arises from the skilled combination of all these elements. This raised awareness is not an end but a means to access a deeper level of self, to cultivate universal truths within. Media corporations have colonized the idea of hip hop by profiting on misogynistic gangsta rap, but this denies the grassroots nature of hip hop, which developed organically on its own in New York's ghettos outside the purview of corporate media or traditional social institutions. Its cut-and-paste aesthetic and artistic innovation presaged the remix and mash-up that has become the dominant motif of internet culture. Despite corporate appropriation, hip hop is still a thriving underground that speaks a poetic language discernable to those who practice its ethics and artistic expression.

Punk and hip hop are among many cultural expressions that model for us an organic approach to a living, transformative media practice. But we now must step up to the planetary emergency that calls upon us to become

Earth-conscious mediators. The very nature of mediation and the capacity to reach across networks around the planet mean that we can become world bridgers. Such a role already exists among indigenous groups. In the mid-1990s an amalgamation of indigenous elders met in Guatemala to organize a concerted response to the world system's encroachment on their cultural survival and living systems. In order to maintain an internal integrity among themselves they agreed that rather than communicate directly with corporations or governments, they would work with *chakaruna* to liase with the outside world. *Chakaruna,* "bridge person" in Quechua, is someone with a foot in different worlds, either because she can speak different languages or because she is technically proficient in how the system operates. *Chakaruna* can be lawyers, activists, artists, politicians, teachers, scholars, media makers, or those who engage in any activity that directly links the worlds of indigenous people and the system they work in. Chakaruna can also be shaman.

An inspiring example of a kind of wizard that bridges tradition and technology is the Andean *yachachiq*. Over the past five thousand years the Quechua of the Andes have maintained and developed highly successful agricultural systems, with *yachachiqs* serving as the technical experts who disseminate and innovate knowledge. The Quechua culture, which doesn't distinguish between art and technique, assigns special status for those who combine technical and creative skills. In the spirit of DIY they serve their communities, helping them remain resilient and self-sufficient.

They maintain an indigenous perspective of land and community while also adapting and working with appropriate technology. The *yachachiq* models a kind of organic media practice, because technical skills are shared through teaching and communicating in different communities in order to promote cultural resiliency.

In our quest for media solutions and futuristic communication strategies using the latest technologies, it behooves us to also tap into those traditions that have excelled under the most dire and genocidal policies of colonization. Whether it's the Hopi maintaining their ancient ceremonial traditions, *chakaruna* bridging with the world system, *yachachiq* engaging appropriate technology, or modern youths seeking authentic cultural expression, these kinds of activities are all part of the same sacred hoop that ties media practice to the ancient future.

Organic Media Ethics

Combining the insights of indigenous peoples with organic subcultures like punk or hip hop results in an ethical framework for media practice that calls for a new kind of accountability that eschews colonial values. Indeed, the DIY ethic that arises organically within subcultures is an effort to empower communities and promote self-determination in response to the domination of corporate media and popular culture. Whereas the corporate colonial paradigm tries to enforce dependency and passivity through the promotion of consumer culture, claiming a space and producing media that expresses the interests of our communities is a necessary step toward building vibrant, resilient, and alternative cultures that no longer feed the carnivorous desires of the corporatocracy. It's heartening that, increasingly, the daily use of internet media and social platforms has DIY and community making as its default practice. What now needs to happen is to make that engagement ecologically conscious so that these activities extend to the concerns of living systems. In short, this calls for a kind of green cultural citizenship.

In order to engage in green cultural citizenship, it's important to follow several key principles:

- *All life is sacred.* This universal cultural ethic transcends the imperatives of a world system that sees life as an instrument of commerce and wealth accumulation. Media can no longer disassociate humans from this principle. This is a core attitude of green cultural citizenship.

- *We are all interconnected.* The idea of the autonomous individual disconnected from nature and culture is a modern invention of the Industrial-Scientific Revolution. Such disconnected reasoning has led to the dangerous concept that corporations are also individuals with rights above the interests of the global community and living systems. In reality we learn, evolve, and grow through a shared cultural commons accessible to everyone. Private media monopolies, enclosure of intellectual property, and the promotion of individualism are unacceptable behaviors in a planetary commons.

■ *As interconnected beings, we depend on functional communities.* We live and participate in communities of scale—from the local to the planetary. At each level we are responsible for our actions, which means engaging the world as citizens instead of mere consumers. Media designed solely on the principle of consumption and markets has little to contribute to the evolution and survival of planetary communities.

■ *Communities require healthy communication to function well.* The key to successful relationships is transparency. Humans need to communicate with each other in order to solve problems. A green cultural citizenship represents diverse voices and egalitarian principles at its core. It respects interhuman essences—such as freedom of expression, dignity, social responsibility, gender and racial equity, and human rights.

■ *For healthy communication to work we need trust.* Accountability, truthfulness, respect, authenticity, and integrity are essential qualities for green cultural citizenship.

■ *Trust requires credibility and reciprocity.* An attitude of generosity is the underlying spiritual posture of decolonized media. It means encouraging sharing, openness, cooperation, and nonviolence, and discourages fear and the enclosure of the cultural commons. Genuine reciprocity builds credible and authentic relationships.

CHAPTER 2

Mediating the World System

Through a shrewd mix of sex, violence, disaster, shock, and fear propagated through its media channels, the world system sells us the antidote to its own chaos through a religion of consumption and economic growth. Six massive multinational corporations monopolize the global media space, promising instant gratification and magical transformation through commodities, fetishizing those very objects that are destroying our living habitats. As it dynamites mountaintops, extracts tar from sands, toxifies waterways, acidifies the oceans, and chokes oxygen from our air, it declares that all of this is necessary for the sake of business as usual. Like the ancient god of the Old Testament, it also asks us to perform ritual sacrifice, first by sending our children to war, and second by destroying living systems on its behalf. It can take many forms, but if you are attuned to its true nature, the world system can't hide its destructive capacity.

Right now the game is on to convert whatever wisdom, creativity, and attention we have left into energy for the world system. To this insidious force, you are just food. It stalks you with increasingly greater means of electronic surveillance, even when it's "innocently" in the form of market research or data-mining social networks. Unbeknownst to our friends and family, many are being recruited and incorporated into this world-eating mechanism, occupying our lifeworld like an invasion of the body snatchers.

Evidence of the emerging world system can be found throughout history. But if you try to identify the leader or a specific ideology, it will be difficult. Is it capitalism, patriarchy, alienation, monotheism? More aptly it is mental and spiritual confusion projected into elaborate systems, becoming an ecology of "bad ideas" normalized through institutions, communication networks, education, religion, and language that shape culture. In this way the world system depends on colonial media to infiltrate our lifeworld.

Information Cartels

Technically *media* is the plural form of *medium,* a medium being something that *mediates* communication. Strictly speaking, T-shirts, graffiti stencils, satellite TV, sports stadiums, baby photos, and YouTube videos of stupid animal tricks are examples of media. But in everyday parlance, the massive multinational institutions and the technological infrastructure that facilitate the majority of mediated communications in our everyday surroundings are often spoken of as a singular entity, The Media, or what activists call Big Media. In this sense, the media as a totality is a space of action and appearance shared by anyone who has access to it.

Consequently, a major outcome of the globalization project has been the creation of a planetary communications commons, best represented by the internet. Such a commons remains out of reach to many of the world's populations. However, with increased access, growing use of cell phones, and the integration of regional media systems into global networks—such as the Qatar-based TV network Al Jazeera—people increasingly are linked together into a mesh of complex associations. This shared space can be likened to a semiosphere, the semiotic equivalent of the biosphere, in which various symbol systems create interacting ecologies of meaning. But since media systems are not just a collection of symbols—they are also technological environments that afford different experiences—ultimately the mediasphere is a kind of information ecology that mixes both symbolic and technological environments. And just as environmentalists address the state of the biosphere, we should be media environmentalists that look at sustainability as a problem of the cultural commons and how corporations have colonized the mediasphere.

Curiously, one of the greatest ironies of the globalized media commons is how it connects and disconnects us simultaneously. Symbolically media bring us closer to aspects of the world we normally don't have access to, yet media also keep us at a physical distance. Media critics have noted that images have a way of "thingifying" reality so that we come to identify representations as real. What we see mediated becomes our reference point for cultures we don't know or understand; meanwhile, these symbolic representations distance us physically and psychologically from the source.

Even though the internet expands the planetary cultural commons, we need to be mindful of symbolic diversity. One of the by-products of the planetary media environment is the potential loss of an indigenous, Earth-based perspective grounded in place-based experience and interaction with organic, living systems. For this reason we need to highlight how the modern media system evolved and has traditionally excluded indigenous perspectives. At the same time, we can also acknowledge that a space exists, and examples abound, in which media are repurposed by Earth-based peoples. Ultimately, as author Jeremy Rifkin argues, media enable us to extend our natural capacity to empathize with others. Global networks move us beyond the religious and national identities that characterized the rise of Western culture so that we can see humanity and the biosphere as a whole.

Media Affect

Media affect is what we do with media; *media effects* is what media does to us. Rather than as something "out there" and beyond our reach, media actually move through us. The people's microphone used during Occupy Wall Street makes this point more clearly. Because voice amplification was banned by the police, to compensate during daily meetings (called General Assemblies) speakers' words were repeated by participants so that people far away could hear. As the communication literally moved through people, these protestors repurposed the ritual aspects of face-to-face communication. Yet these oral media encounters were also being hybridized by technology. Techie activists developed smartphone apps that allowed orators to be heard live by phone, thereby turning each phone into a mini-megaphone. Moreover, through live streaming on the internet, these voices extended far beyond the local assemblies to an international audience. Those watching the stream could also participate through typing comments.

The media economy works on the principle that if it's free, you are the product. What we watch, pay attention to, or create online is sold to marketers. Without our active response via our attention, media products have no value. Thus, key to the media economy is how "affect" moves through people. In the one-to-many system of industrial, top-down media production, affect is measured by circulation (newspapers), audience ratings (radio and TV), and sales (concert and film tickets, books, recordings, DVDs, etc.). In such a system there is very low feedback between consumers and producers, but feedback exists. In the current many-to-many system empowered by social networks on the internet, media affect is measured by what we share and whom we share it with. Whether or not that activity gets commodified depends on the kind of media ecosystems we engage. From a dystopian perspective, though social media enable greater feedback, we inadvertently commodify ourselves by allowing companies to profit from our interests and relationships. From a utopian perspective, we become a human web through which planetary consciousness can weave itself. The difference between the two means disentangling the prerogatives of the world system from this web and engaging in green cultural citizenship.

The world system is reproduced through "colonial media," the traditional information cartels dominated by the likes of AT&T, NBC-Comcast, Disney, and News Corp., many of which emerged as a direct consequence of technological and electrical cartels that began forming in the nineteenth century. Colonial media are part and parcel of the contemporary globalization project. Globalization is hardly new or neutral. Mostly it's postmodern colonialism masked by educated vandals that network and tether us into its complex web of electricity in service of global finance.

Whether using highways, airwaves, or telecommunications, in order for media cartels to communicate to the general public they depend on a commonly shared infrastructure. As private corporations, media cartels are licensed by "the people" to conduct business. Unfortunately, rather than engage in a quid pro quo with the public—we allow them to conduct business in exchange for respecting the public good—the cartels continue to enclose our shared resources. Enclosure is the legal seizure of the commons, as was the case in England when commonly shared peasant lands were fenced off and privatized. The primary economic model of colonial media is to enclose the cultural commons through intellectual property laws, monopolization, and control of the technological infrastructure.

Emerging cartels in the form of new media corporations like Facebook and Google are now being absorbed—eaten, really—by this system, though their character and style are different: they wear flip flops, use words like "cool," and say things like "don't be evil." Yes, the tools are great and have contributed greatly to the spread of information and making it easier for people to connect. These benefits will be discussed more below, but for now it remains to be seen whether or not we can trust these benevolent dictatorships to be friends of open systems, democracy, privacy, free speech, living systems, and the cultural commons. On the surface, new media are participatory and emancipatory, but the fundamental economic model of traditional and emerging media systems is the same: if it's free, you are the product. Venture capitalists that drive these platforms are not culturally neutral. Given a choice, they'd rather sell you an app for democracy than actually build a democratic society that is ecologically just.

Consider the typical smartphone, with its environmental and labor costs externalized and borne by folks less lucky then the average user. These phones are made possible through the extraction of conflict minerals (such as coltan or tantalum) in Africa, fueling civil war, rape, and child labor. Its components contain highly contaminating chemicals. After being assembled in China by humans that have been turned into machine parts, it is shipped overseas with atmosphere-contaminating emissions. Its components, when disposed of, poison workers and water supplies and cause air pollution. As a portal for our attention, we pay a heavy financial price—the cost of the device and service fees to the information cartels are heavy rents. During Steve Jobs's reign at Apple, environmental and worker concerns were often rejected for the sake of expedience. Yet these devices are marketed as something pure, a force of good, a means to connect with one another, a form of personal expression, a conduit of cultural citizenship, a necessary product for the advancement of civilization. All of these cultural by-products are certainly meaningful, but decontextualized from the circuit of energy consumption and waste, these cultural attributes become moot. When springs are poisoned and the food chain is disrupted irreparably, data will not nourish our bodies. We cannot survive by eating information. But technology companies and information cartels survive by eating us.

In terms of telecommunications technology, when companies like Apple set out to create amazing gadgets that facilitate creativity, media making, and communication, they usually fail to be holistic in their approach. They make choices that discriminate between consumers and workers, rich and poor, technology and the environment. In the traditional media system, consumers just accept the status quo without challenge. But the growing Green IT movement, which seeks to "green" technology, cannot share information or ideas without using existing technologies, nor can the peer-to-peer paradigm get enacted without building on current conditions. What's heartening is that a number of technologies and platforms are transitioning into a participatory paradigm. IBM uses

Linux, major artists use Creative Commons, Google uses open APIs, and a slew of new communication platforms depend on user input and sharing.

The point is not whether or not we should abandon telecommunications technology or corporate media, but how we can do better and reappropriate them to advance social change. *Avatar*'s blue-hued natives, the Na'vi, and the Guy Fawkes mask from *V for Vendetta* are both trademarked images from corporate media, yet they are symbolically repurposed by activists. Consider these as examples of media homeopathy, which is the practice of taking small doses of poison in order to build up our immunity. Culture jammers and pranksters use media as an artistic medium and means for critique. Cultural citizenship seeks to transform daily practice, economics, and design. We need everyone to become a cultural citizen who agitates for sustainable and just media and technology. Rather than becoming technological separatists or isolationists, I believe engagement is the best way to effect change.

Uncommon Sense

Every system has tension points and contradictions. How these stress points get resolved indicates the system's resilience. The world system survives by a process that many call *hegemony*, the practice of naturalizing the system's ideology so that its unequal economic structure becomes common sense. We're not talking about "common sense" in the practical use of the phrase, such as making sensible decisions about how we react to situations. Rather, it refers to what we accept as the "normal" condition of reality. For the world system, thinking like an extraterrestrial is common sense.

Hegemony replicates itself through various means of consent. People acquire it through the complex affordances of everyday life: social relationships, education, financial means, work, religion, etc. There are four important principles to understand about hegemony: 1) culture is not neutral; 2) cultural choices have political consequences; 3) hegemony is flexible, and therefore can respond to cultural change; and 4) hegemony's flexibility is a sign that people do in fact resist and contest dominant ideologies. Indeed, corporate media are very adept at channeling the anxieties and tensions within society. For example, *The Simpsons,* which is broadcast on Fox, often pokes fun at Fox News and deals with a variety of social issues. In one episode, it commissioned street artist and prankster Banksy to storyboard its opening couch gag. Banksy satirizes the animated series as part of an exploitive global system, mocking how the show is animated in Korea and its merchandise is manufactured under exploitative conditions in China. Nonetheless, the world system's incredible plasticity enables it to survive these challenges to its dominion. Inevitably corporate media, whether expressed in the form of comedy or Hollywood cinema, wrangles with social anxieties but also offers its own pat solutions through consumerism or conventional plot resolutions. It remains to be seen if the world system can survive by eating its planetary host alive, but up to now, resistance has been relatively futile. Like the Borg in the *Star Trek* series, it can incorporate and co-opt just about anyone and any point of view. The fact that in the United States many consider climate change a hoax perpetuated by radical environmentalists highlights this depressing dynamic. However, as will be explained in the last chapter, the motif of powerlessness propagated by both the left and right is being undermined by an emergent planetary revolution. Nonetheless, it's best to map the challenges faced by such movements.

Hegemony is like a sun at the center of a solar system of ideas: it draws everything into its orbit, defining alternative points of view in relationship to its gravitational pull. A past example includes how the Roman Catholic Church could define the nature of the cosmos and eliminate alternative viewpoints. But ultimately it was no match for the Industrial-Scientific Revolution that supplanted it and gave rise to the corporatocracy. Right now hegemony's center of gravity is based on a convergence between information cartels, centralized energy monopolies, consolidated financial trusts, multinational corporations (food, pharmaceuticals, mining), and the global security state that shores up the planetary corporatocracy. In the short run, for these groups, this is a very "successful" system. A small number of people are getting very, very, very rich from it. Like trolls, they thrive on other people's misery and can only succeed in conditions of chaos. The Sustainability Revolution will eventually replace this system, but until it becomes the center of our collective attention, we will have to develop alternative practices that not only discredit the current system but make the emergent paradigm attractive and necessary.

Can convergence and the participatory culture arising with new media practices challenge hegemony? Predictably, traditional capitalist media adapt and co-opt emerging media trends through enclosure and also by mimicking their practices. Obviously, Super Bowl ads constructed through user-generated media do not represent consumer democracy. If the choices remain limited and the fundamental assumptions of the system go unchallenged by new cultural practices, then we will get "interpassivity"—philosopher Slavoj Žižek's tongue-in-cheek poke at the popular notion that interactivity automatically leads to greater participation. Again, we need to be careful that our belief in networks doesn't become another kind of magical thinking propagated by the world system to make us believe that the internet will automatically lead to utopia, let alone a true Earth Democracy. After all, organized crime, hate groups, terrorists, spammers, identity thieves, child pornographers, slave traders, dictatorships, militaries, and nefarious corporations also use the net for their ends. No freedom comes automatically without struggle and oppositional politics.

Neoliberalism

The primary framework that drives the economics of globalization is neoliberalism. This may seem obvious to the educated and informed, but surprisingly few people actually know what neoliberalism is about. In a nutshell it means unregulated businesses, promoting free markets, and the increased enclosure of the cultural commons. There are four current trends to be aware of: privatization and commodification, financialization, using crisis as an instrument of control, and redistribution of wealth from the public sector to the private. Media cartels play an important role because as transnational corporations they are integral to the process of neoliberal economics. If sustainability means consuming less and reversing economic "growth," these ideas are contrary to the financial structure of media that depend on the promotion of consumerism and privatization for their obscene profits. Rupert Murdoch's News Corp. (owner of Fox News), for example, uses its media to push the neoliberal ideology out of self-interest, not because it's a moral philosophy. General Electric, a principle owner of NBC, also owns financial institutions and makes weapons. The board members of the major media cartels are interlinked with the government and finance system to the point that beneath the surface such a system mimics the behavior of fascism. Subsequently, with little critique from major media corporations, the powers behind neoliberalism are doubling down their insanity: despite the potential of a runaway climate crisis demanding more than ever that corporations be reigned in, regulations are weakened, treaties broken, and international negotiations stalled. Clearly we have reached a crisis in democracy.

Luckily, opposing this fascist integration of corporate and hyper-militarized nation-states is what the political philosophers Antonio Negri and Michael Hardt call the "networked power" of the global multitudes, who are developing alternative forms of social coordination and articulating new forms of response to the system of global domination. In recent years we have seen this in the Middle East, in the protests in Greece and Spain, in the riots in London and the Occupy movement. As the stakes get higher, the production of decolonized media becomes that much more crucial: in a globally networked world such as our own, new ideas and memes, new images of alternative utopias, and new methods of resistance and organizational strategies can be disseminated more easily. The rising power of these movements was evidenced when *Time* magazine named the protestor as their 2011 person of the year. It is a sure sign that the ideas expressed by the ill-defined global protest movement are resonating in popular culture in such a way that they cannot be ignored by traditional corporate media. The *Time* cover design itself was made by Shepard Fairey, a veteran punk and skateboarder whose guerrilla street art has achieved pop culture status. As will be discussed, the specific alternative media strategies of these protestors has insured that their activities are present within the global media commons.

Nonetheless, it is important to be watchful and to choose partners wisely. Media services used by protestors are largely unregulated and are integral to the neoliberal system of globalization. Though Google and Facebook have certainly enabled people to self-organize, they are also not public services and have at times acted out of self-interest, endangering the lives of activists. For example, in many countries anonymity is a crucial protection against police and state repression. Activists at times have been exposed or deleted from crucial online groups due to the anonymity policies of these private companies. Without clear policies, such as ensuring an open internet, closing the digital divide, public funding for commercial free communications spaces, and an internet bill of rights, many of our activities—and their safety from government intrusion and surveillance—will depend on the goodwill of private corporations. As WikiLeaks learned in 2010, when online services such as Amazon.com, PayPal, and MasterCard either blocked WikiLeaks or disallowed people to contribute money to the organization, censorship can be privatized. If our cultural commons continues to be privatized, it will be more difficult for alternative media and information sources to exist and do their work.

Control Mechanisms

In the 1950s, when it became clear that TV and mass media were integral to the rise of a new economic order in which consumerism would drive the postwar global economy, the sociologist C. Wright Mills astutely observed, "Those who rule the management of symbols rule the world." Symbolic control is one of the greatest battles taking place before our very eyes, yet most have no clue that there is a war going on at all. All symbols exist in relation to power. The most obvious example is 9/11. The feelings and images connected to it are shaped through a very intensive propaganda effort that ensures that certain interpretations are consistent. The meaning of the Twin Towers crashing down is closely tied to patriotism and the so-called war on terror. A more innocuous example, yet one that is very potent, is any image associated with technology. We relate a host of values, economic policies, identity issues, and political stances with what we believe about technology, whether in the form of cars, computers, satellites, or aircraft carriers. How is the meaning of these symbols enforced?

A propaganda system has evolved that ensures that certain ruling ideas prevail through a five-pronged method: media monopoly, advertising, reliance on government sources, bullying, and fearmongering. The sheer size of the media cartels makes them heavily dependent on the status quo: to maintain the functioning of the system they benefit from, they will squash and suppress innovation or competing ideas. For example, based on its policy not to air controversial advocacy spots, in 2008 Disney's ABC network wouldn't run an ad by Repower America that linked climate change with the petroleum economy. Concurrently, dependence on advertising—in particular rich advertisers such as automakers—means that the underlying assumptions of "growth," "progress," "consumerism," and "technology" will rarely, if ever, be challenged.

Confronting these primary cultural assumptions is sacrilegious, and I don't say that to be polemical. These beliefs are akin to religious doctrine. This is even the case with critical comedy shows like *The Daily Show* and *The Colbert Report*. While it's true that these programs offer more critique of media than anywhere else in the offerings of the media cartels, the very fact that their criticism is contextualized as irony and comedy means that we can maintain emotional distance from critical issues without having to act on them. They serve as pressure valves that give the appearance that oppositional viewpoints are tolerated. Indeed, hegemony creates space for critique and alternative cultural practices, as long as they can be absorbed and contained within nonthreatening perimeters.

Accordingly, in mainstream media bullying is used to keep people in line. Reporters, pundits, managers, and programmers act as shock troops to make sure the essential tenets of the system are never challenged. Presenters at Fox News, for instance, use neuro-linguistic programming techniques to frame and discredit any views that challenge the prevailing ideology of business as usual. Like magicians, through timed hand gestures, body language, and carefully choreographed word usage, media personnel, politicians, and pop artists conjure thought forms to shape perception.

Bullying could be seen in the corporate media's initial response to the recent Occupy movement. As is the case with any activism that challenges the status quo going back to the 1960s, corporate media would typically marginalize the protestors' claims through flak. They discredited these claims through association with the counterculture ("they're not like us," "they are not reasonable people," "they are lunatics") and radicals ("anarchists," "socialists," "communists," "Hamas affiliates," "anti-Semites," "Nazis," etc.). They imposed a narrative that portrayed the protestors as childlike ("petulant," "spoiled"), ignorant ("they don't know what they want"), aiding the enemy (Hugo Chavez, Hamas, and Iranians "love them"), and destructive ("they want our stuff," "they will destroy capitalism"). This is not to say that sympathizers in the corporate media don't exist. Indeed, when it was clear that Occupy resonated with mainstream Americans, many in the corporate media offered more sympathetic coverage. Nonetheless, those seeking a serious discourse about the world's problems won't find much of it in a media environment dominated by conflict-driven infotainment spectacles that consider shouting matches to be democratic debates.

The strategy of marginalization and demonization by the corporate media is old news, of course, and easily anticipated. The key difference now—compared to, say, in 1968 when anti-war activists getting beaten by cops in Chicago chanted, "The whole world is watching"—is the changed dynamic between consumers and producers of news. The past was dominated by a top-down media structure ruled by gatekeepers who decided "All the news that's fit to print," or could declare at the end of the newscast, "And that's the way it is." The Occupiers largely self-mediated, thereby eschewing a narrative that could easily be manipulated and coerced. Based on a Twitter hashtag (#occupywallstreet, #ows), it disseminated horizontally. The whole world wasn't watching—it was streaming. The

Occupiers' innovative strategies and workarounds demonstrated the capacity for human intelligence to circumvent dominator power structures.

Media companies, which are regulated by the government—in other words, the government on behalf of the people gives permission for these companies to do business—engage in unspoken quid pro quo. (I'll scratch your back if you'll scratch mine.) There are numerous cases of government pressure on private media companies to withhold information, and the capitulation of editors who fear losing access or upsetting the powers that be. For example, despite clear evidence that the post–9/11 invasion of Iraq was an oil war, it was never discussed as such and was always framed within the perimeters defined by the government. The reportage of the *New York Times* was so negligent and atrocious that it eventually wrote an apology and practically retracted its uncritical reporting of the government's arguments leading up to the war. In other cases, media companies have withdrawn or withheld controversial programming prior to key votes regarding how their businesses are regulated.

Fearmongering through "official" enemies defines the range of debate about how issues are discussed. In the past it was anti-communism, though you will still see this alive and well at Fox News. Depending on the venue, presently enemies range from "Islamofascists," "radical" environmentalists, unions, immigrants, and copyright pirates to Occupy protestors. Most ridiculously, those threatening the status quo are accused of advocating class warfare.

But as media activists have pointed out, those who make accusations of class warfare are actually the ones waging it.

These basic control mechanisms comprise what Edward S. Herman and Noam Chomsky refer to as the "propaganda model." When it comes to climate change, this model has been particularly effective in reversing the trend toward increased public sympathy for environmental concerns. In recent years, the importance of the environment has been usurped by the economic crisis. This is not surprising given that capitalism as a kind of religious dogma in the United States is utterly undermined by the reality of climate change. The solutions necessary to address the planetary ecological emergency mean that we must essentially dismantle the dominant industrial paradigm of the past two centuries. Corporate media, up to now at least, have not significantly confronted the reality of what our current moment calls for. Whether it's the weak and ineffectual coverage of global climate change negotiations, the perpetuation of the growth model in news programing and advertising schemes, the framing of the economy as indifferent to ecology, the marginalization of climate science as an anti-capitalist conspiracy, the ability of the fossil fuel industry to game the political system and news cycle, or the lack of alternative perspectives, the most powerful media companies in the world essentially have abdicated morality in exchange for the short-term satisfaction of anthropocentric domination of the world.

Teacher Function

How does the world system train us? Here's one example. A Direct TV advertisement for its satellite service begins with a boy in a living room watching TV with his father, sometime in the 1950s. The child moves into other rooms, each time getting older as he enters into a new era, always accompanied by TV. It ends with him on a couch with his grandson, watching, of course, TV. Accompanied by magical lullaby music—the kind typical of fantasy movies like the Harry Potter films—its narrator is familiar to us from the MasterCard commercials. In a comforting voice he speaks of TV in grand philosophical terms: it's a portal, a mirror, a doorway. The ad is very self-referential: it does the very things it promises TV will do for us. It teaches us what is normal by showing us that common people are middle class, white suburbanites. As an advertisement it services the economic system by selling us a product that is primarily financed by marketing. By depicting its protagonist as a soldier during the 1960s, it shows how TV is a venue for politics. TV also surveys the world, depicted by the images shown on the TVs in the background: the moon walk and Mark McGwire's chase of Roger Maris's home run record. Throughout the ad people look to TV for entertainment and interpretation of the world.

All of these elements combined highlight how TV functions as a teaching medium, one that not only coordinates behavior but also instructs us how the world works. By not calling itself an educational device, it actually becomes more powerful than the education system. We let down our guards and engage it informally, allowing it to subtly teach us what to care about. More precisely, it doesn't teach what to think, but what to think about.

When it comes to understanding media, TV, of course, is not the whole picture. But it continues to maintain a pervasive and ubiquitous presence in our lives. Despite the increasing popularity of the internet, TV remains the king of media. A conduit of over $9 billion a year spent on advertising, TV is the primary communication medium for the world system. Some argue that the internet will replace TV, but so far that hasn't happened. In the U.S. TV still has higher penetration into households than broadband. Efforts to integrate TV with the internet have failed repeatedly because they do different things. Nonetheless traditional media companies have hybridized themselves with the internet and have successfully colonized much of it. The major internet news portals, for example, are dominated by media cartels, such as MSNBC, CNN, and AOL. YouTube's most watched videos are of artists represented by traditional multinational media companies.

TV teaches us an important lesson about education. We are not formally taught how to watch TV, but we acquire our ability to understand and make sense of it informally. We take it for granted that all the discontinuities, juxtapositions of close-ups and long shots, flashing edits, and narrative disruptions would be difficult to understand for someone that has never encountered the medium before. The conventions of editing that emerged during the early days of film did not come naturally to audiences. Cross-cutting between different events and scenes, for example, initially didn't make sense. People learned informally to understand it by imposing a kind of metanarrative amidst the clutter, channel surfing, divergent story lines, and juxtapositions. Over time and through repeated exposure, certain beliefs become "cultivated," the simplest being that commodities have magical properties to transform our lives, the other being that the world is a dangerous place and can only be stabilized by war, technology, pharmaceuticals, and commodities.

Most importantly, the aforementioned Direct TV ad is an argument that the cultural commons should be enclosed by crass marketing and commercial exploitation. In the 1980s the so-called postmodern aesthetic (as epitomized by MTV's blurring of advertising, art, and programming) was the subject of debate and criticism. Whether people were critical or celebratory of the rise of postmodernism, they still thought like modernists, which meant that cultural boundaries had significance and people believed in the distinction between art and economics, or between politics and marketing. This, of course, is a romanticized version of history because the boundaries had long been crossed, but the culture at large still held taboos against crossing certain lines, in particular the commercialization of music. It wasn't until the Beatles' song "Revolution" appeared in a Nike ad in 1987 (against the wishes of the living members of the Beatles) that a threshold was crossed which elevated "selling out" to social acceptability. Nowadays it's hard to imagine a world without product placement—the discreet and not-so-discreet injection of products into film scripts, TV shows, and pop music. With hypertext and contextual ads, the internet is a de facto postmodern space; those native to it simply have not lived through the debates about how this impacts culture. Distinguishing between a sales pitch and genuine communication has become increasingly difficult. This is particularly challenging for activists who develop creative media strategies, like flash mobs, only to see them turned into a guerrilla marketing strategy. The repeated mining of innovative communication strategies shows the length by which the world system will appropriate authentic human experiences and repackage them into commodities.

Fortunately, by engaging emerging media ecosystems, media users of today informally learn new ways of being that are increasingly more participatory. Just as TV is pedagogical, the internet and its various emergent social practices "teach" us new cultural behaviors. In many ways participatory media practices challenge the old order by instilling an expectation of transparency, collaboration, participation, and sharing, all key ingredients for horizontal democracy. Will new media users, then, de facto evolve a decolonized mentality? Not necessarily. In order to maintain a posture of hope, we need to be mindful of the world system's shape-shifting capacity. Vigilance, mindfulness, and literacy for how these tools have the duel nature of serving both increased democracy and corporate control are necessary to ensure that the great potential of communication tools doesn't become a lost opportunity.

Convergence

The rise of convergence culture shows how the boundaries between traditional and networked media have created positive conditions for increased participation and cultural citizenship. Unlike traditional mass media, which had low levels of interactivity and feedback, networked media have altered the equation significantly. But convergence culture is not the same as convergence media, which explains the invasion of the internet by media cartels (remember the internet was initially a public space created by governments and universities and funded by taxpayers). The former is about cultural practice and the latter relates to the convergence of devices, platforms, and content producers. The two are interrelated, but they don't necessarily share the same goals. Convergence culture is driven by emergent grassroots movements, innovative programmers, fans, entrepreneurs, and users that drive innovation through their need to communicate and interact, whereas convergence media are driven by the logic of adaptation curves, venture capital, technological integration, and monopolization. In both cases cultural practice and economics can veer between open and closed systems.

Henry Jenkins's model of convergence culture is characterized by four trends: collective intelligence, affective economics, transmedia storytelling, and participatory culture. In the commercial realm, an example of these four trends can be applied to the pop culture sensation *Lost*. Broadcast on Disney's TV network, ABC (2004–2010), initially it was a traditional media offering in that it was produced for a large mass audience on a set time during the weekly programming schedule. But its appearance coincided with the rise of the web, iTunes, and peer-to-peer sharing. The normal distribution channels were supplemented by ABC's re-broadcast on its website, individual shows were sold through iTunes, and one could also get episodes via file sharing technologies like BitTorrent. As the program grew in popularity, fans started to comment and collectively work to solve the various puzzles that were built into the show's innovative story arc. The producers intentionally designed the show with gaming motifs that made the show interactive. Their strategy of transmedia storytelling meant that the storyline was extended across the web, video games, books, and DVDs.

Rising social networks like MySpace became venues for discussions about the show's mysteries, exemplifying collective intelligence. Fan videos started to appear on YouTube, an expression of affective economics and participatory culture. Affective economics means engaging activities out of love for the brand. Fans were willing to share and spread the *Lost* brand without expecting anything in return except for the chance to extend the experience of joy they got from the program. The producers, in turn, became obliged and tethered to their fans, thereby creating a far more interactive relationship than was available with industrial-era media.

By the final season, an interesting manifestation of these practices occurred in Italy. Two groups of voluntary translators began competing for who could subtitle the latest episode the quickest. Within minutes of the TV broadcast in North America, a digital version of the show was uploaded to file sharing networks. Translation crews in Italy downloaded them, working feverishly to get the episodes re-uploaded with Italian subtitles, usually within twenty-four hours. Such practices undermine the licensing of shows in foreign territories and impact DVD sales of foreign language versions of the program, but they also strengthen the title's brand identity. That fans are willing to work so diligently to promote their favorite shows demonstrates that the traditional divide between producer and consumer is increasingly blurred. Moreover, it shows that amateurs are as efficient and mobilized as professional media makers.

But let us not forget that *Lost* is not possible without the big budget production, distribution, and marketing that media cartels like Disney are capable of. *Lost*'s place in our discourse still derives from traditional top-down economics. The vaunted "prosumer"—coined by Alvin Toffler to mean "proactive consumer"—that furthers Disney's brand through fan-made mash-ups creates the appearance of increased democratic participation, but it's still centered around products made by media cartels. The concern is that such celebrated fan culture is often thoroughly colonized by corporations, because ultimately media companies remain the arbiters of the product's intellectual property, and they muscle websites like YouTube by making copyright violation claims against users who don't follow the producers' rules.

This was the case with the Star Wars franchise, which at first tightly controlled and restricted fan-made media, but eventually loosened up a bit to give fans a venue to make their re-interpretations of the films. Currently fans are not allowed to use the copyrighted characters, but they can create their own stories within the Star Wars universe. This seems like a reasonable compromise between the desire of the creator to maintain some control over how a work is reinterpreted and loyal fans who want to personalize their experience with the brand. On the other hand, this compromise disregards the fact that fan films are a kind of folk culture, and that once certain ideas and stories enter into the public domain, they become part of our common heritage. Such is the tension of modern storytelling. Our symbols are continually struggled over as the goals and interests of intellectual property control conflict with the needs of the culture to dialogue and incorporate those artifacts of daily life into forms of personal and social expression.

In the activist realm, convergence culture was exemplified by the practices of the Occupy movement. Collective intelligence and participatory practices were reflected in the horizontal character of the movement. Whether it was through physical presence at General Assemblies or through participation on online forums, the movement glocalized planetary activism through seizing public and virtual spaces to repurpose democracy. Likewise, through self-mediation, the movement told its story across multiple platforms: physical gatherings, newspapers, websites, live video streams, Tumblr photo blogs, Twitter hashtags, online documentaries, Facebook groups, street demonstrations, and old fashioned cardboard signs. Affective economics was reflected in the very fact that this grassroots movement was funded through donations and voluntary efforts. Though inevitably forces of enclosure will encroach upon the movement through the absorption of its claims into pop culture triviality, or through trademarks by commercial ventures that seek to capitalize on its "brand," it has spread by affect through the planetary cultural commons and people's innate desire to share and link up.

Occupy Sesame Street

If the propaganda model is a direct consequence of media economics, then clearly a decolonized media means financial and energy decolonization. The following anecdote demonstrates how this might be possible.

Soon after the rapid growth of the Occupy movement across the world, a humorous meme emerged on the internet: "Occupy Sesame Street." Images of *Sesame Street* muppet Bert led in handcuffs represented one of many funny and playful takes on the protest movement. But there's also some truth to this meme that resonates with deeper issues of how media are funded. Media ecosystems range from institutions that are state run, publicly subsidized, audience supported, or completely private. In the United States we have mostly a privatized system, with the public licensing of the airwaves for the use of media companies. In the early days of mass media it was a given that for the privilege of using a portion of the airwave commons, media companies had an obligation to contribute to the public good. In England, the British Broadcasting Company was created as a way to bring "culture" to the general public. Since Ronald Reagan and the rise of the neoliberal ideology that seeks to eliminate government regulation, media companies have been allowed to monopolize and converge without regard to public interest.

The most promising and ethically clean funding model exists in the form of audience-supported media. Examples include public community radio; nationally distributed hybrid programs like Democracy Now! that are broadcast on radio, satellite, and the web; online social networks like Evolver (www.evolver.net); oppositional media such as Occupied Wall Street Journal and Independent Media Center (www.indymedia.org); and alternative satellite networks such as Link TV and Free Speech TV, to name just a few. What they have in common is transparency and accountability to their viewers/listeners/readers.

Not surprisingly, when it comes to ethical conflicts, private media suffer far more lapses than public or audience-supported media. The reason is simple. If you compare the ethical guidelines for journalists and marketers, the difference is that journalists are accountable to the public, whereas marketers are accountable to their clients. Since advertisers are the primary patrons of privatized media companies, their ethical orientation is skewed toward the interests of private enterprise. *Sesame Street* is one of the more famous offerings from what little is left of public broadcasting in the United States. Public media are constantly attacked by reactionary politicians in an effort to discipline its producers to be business friendly and uncritical of corporate affairs. As funding dwindles for public media, so does the idea that media are part of the cultural commons. Thus it makes perfect sense from the vantage of media decolonization that we also occupy *Sesame Street,* for it reflects the debate about who the government should be accountable to: taxpayers or tax-dodging corporations.

CHAPTER 3

Media as Environmental Education

Remember, all worldviews are environmental worldviews, whether they are based on exploitation or sustainability. Thus, our ecological emergency is primarily a cultural crisis. Within this context, then, media must be seen as a kind of environmental education. They teach us how to act upon the world, encouraging a particular attitude toward living systems. Media practitioners have a tremendous responsibility to incorporate a more holistic and ecologically intelligent perspective into how they mediate the world. Just as media makers increasingly have become sensitive to the stereotyping of genders, cultures, nationalities, and sexual orientation, we now have to make a turn toward planetary ecology to become aware of how our forms of mediation impact living systems.

Minimarts of the Mind

Our current world system has made the production and reproduction of a certain form of passive, consumerist consciousness its primary product. Subsequently, the world system has colonized the collective unconscious as it preys upon the living world. Following the brilliant

Indian theorist and activist Vandana Shiva, we can understand this system as a mental model, a "monoculture of the mind." Monoculture is an agricultural term for single-crop farming, such as corn, palm oil, or soy, that requires external inputs, like chemical pesticides, petroleum-based fertilizers, and genetically altered seedlings. According to Shiva, monoculture is a "cognitive space," one that sees food or agriculture for what it offers for the market. Whereas a local knowledge-based perspective looks at the nurturing characteristics of a given ecosystem, such as nutrition, soil, water, and life, by contrast a monocultural knowledge system sees ecosystems as resources that can be commoditized, privatized, and controlled. The monocultural approach views life from a rational, scientific perspective. As agriculture, monoculture is not designed for local use or consumption, but for export and transport across the globe. It's mass produced and generic to the point of being without context—it can grow anywhere and be done by anyone who buys into the system (sometimes by choice, sometimes as enforced policy). The monocultural mind has a totalizing effect that extends beyond food systems to larger forms of social and economic organization that expand to the implementation of technology and media. Monoculture has a way of crowding out alternatives in order to promote standardization, masking itself in the rhetoric of development. We categorize nations and people according to whether or not they conform to this "development" scheme. Mass-marketed media are designed to work within this standardized system to the extent that multinational media corporations promote and lobby for laws that favor their products in the global marketplace, protecting their interests against unauthorized uses and competition. They then use media to advocate for their particular position in the marketplace.

To see this phenomenon at work as a coherent system, one only needs to go to a random "convenience" minimart that populates North American highways. These are access points to the monocultural mindset and embody in an extreme way the volatility of the system. Minimarts service the various addictions of our society: oil, alcohol, tobacco, polyunsaturated fats, caffeine, empty carbs, sugar, porn, and packaged media. Some also incorporate fast food kiosks. Here the totalizing spectacle of the world system masks its severe volatility: a breakdown in one key ingredient—oil, either in terms of scarcity or price—crashes the whole system. These portals do not depend on a single local input except for labor and utilities, and even these are often imported. In many poor and rural communities food markets no longer exist, just these vortices of cultural toxins, and as such, they represent monoculture's ideal dream space. Constructed in meadows, clear-cut forest tracts, and on fragile desert soil, each minimart island becomes a desolate outpost of the dominator complex. The misnaming of these portals as "convenient" reveals the anthropocentric and selfish character of unsustainable economic patterns that encourage personal satisfaction over planetary health. Likewise, if global media corporations have their way, the internet and other media distribution channels will become mini-marts of the mind.

Goddess of Light

Advertising is the dream life of corporations. And Pepsi has dreamt up Shakira, a high priestess of the world system. A Colombian-born singer of Lebanese descent, her name means "goddess of light," an appropriate name for someone who is primarily experienced through electricity. Her function became apparent to me around ten years ago when I was working on a media literacy project in northern New Mexico. I was given the task of finding ads for a Spanish-language media and health curriculum that would use media samples to tackle issues like body image, tobacco and alcohol abuse, gender identity, and violence. I taped hours of Spanish-language TV from satellite, hunting for concrete examples of nefarious media to teach with. It wasn't difficult. From underage girls cage dancing on a children's show to mass murdering gangsters strangling women with ropes, Mexican TV is an open laboratory of ritual abuse. But nothing prepared me for what I eventually found.

I missed it on the first run through the tapes. But as I rewatched them, the bleached-blond goddess of the Latin Pop Matrix reasserted herself in a thirty-second spot for Pepsi. Believing at first that this was just a Rorschach test for the litany of social ills I had set out to find, I rewound the commercial over and over again to make sure my senses weren't deceiving me.

The ad opens with a glowing, indigo hued hall exaggerated by linear perspective, as if we are peering beyond the guts of a TV set. Along the frame's edges are circular portal-like windows as if it were the hull of a spacecraft. A concert stage forms the horizon line. Above it hovers a bulbous red, white, and blue sphere. Below the sphere Shakira emerges to face concertgoers. She belts a jingle devoted to global freedom, stalking along a cat walk, slithering, cooing, teasing her way toward the camera. Then a long shot reveals the stage's actual shape: a crucifix. The portal windows now resemble stained glass windows, and long columns look eerily like the pillars of a great cathedral. If you are Latin American and Roman Catholic, the allusion is unmistakable. Shakira is performing Mass.

As the concert progresses, her moves are ritualistically mirrored by an audience of clean-cut, adoring youth. In the final shot a Pepsi bottle materializes in Shakira's hand, appearing from a flash of light. Shakira, and then the crowd of teen followers, together imbibe the Black Water of Imperialism. In sync they perform a transubstantiation of the world system: the indigenous colonized are transformed and purified by the Blood of Capitalism in order to go to Heaven to become White People.

As a spiritual sermon, here the world system represents itself as the dominant planetary religion. The advertisement is a mini-ritual designed to educate Latin Americans that in order to better their lives, they must transform themselves into what Shakira has become. She had already altered her identity to join the planetary cult: she transitioned from her once dark-haired and distinct Latina identity to a blond angelic archetype typical of world system media: an succubus. Like her predecessors Britney Spears, Christina Aguilera, and Madonna, she is a leather-clad, blond vixen set out to train youths to become proper aliens. Her divinity is bequeathed by the red, white, and blue sphere. Like the pied piper, she beckons youth to leave behind their traditions in order to board her fun-filled spacecraft. To transform ourselves from the old world into the new, the magical, transformative elixir is, of course, Pepsi.

Where's the Beef?

In addition to soda, corporate media and hamburgers have a lot in common. They succeed because they stimulate the pleasure centers of our brains. As an example of how they converge, in 2008 Burger King launched a viral marketing campaign called "Whopper Virgins." The idea was to take the Whopper burger to remote regions of the world and to film how people reacted to it in a taste "test" against the McDonald's Big Mac.

To create the campaign, Burger King enlisted skater/filmmaker Stacy Peralta, director of *Dogtown* and *Z Boys,* which documented the skater counterculture in LA during the 1970s. He took a crew to Thailand, Romania, and Greenland where he filmed in mockumentary style. It has all the signs of a legitimate documentary by using shaky cameras, interviews, and "realism," but to any keen-eyed, media-literate observer it was clearly a farce. It portrayed the North American film crew as "normal" in order to make the regional cultures appear absurd and strange, a technique going back to early circuses. The crew describes the hamburger as if it were a kind of religious article of faith; of course anyone should like it and adapt their culture to it. Not only that, it should be Burger King that provides the access point to this product.

In terms of promoting green consciousness, hamburgers are one of the least ecologically sustainable food products. Making them requires an obscene amount of natural resources, from water to clear-cutting forests for ranch lands. Moreover, hamburger production is highly automated, technological, and centralized. For these reasons the hamburger is closely tied to climate change and symbolizes perfectly the monocultural mindset.

In order to propagate the hamburger, the ad campaign needs to scramble our common sense. It does this through its pseudo claim to authenticity by incorporating Peralta's street cred and fake documentary style to give it a sense of verisimilitude—a feeling of "reality." The growth of reality TV techniques is not confined to TV programming but also extends to marketing and viral media. This demonstrates how corporate media survive by eating reality: whenever possible they have to harvest shreds of the real to claim legitimacy. It's a very sketchy, sneaky, and unethical game. But that is what is afoot.

Monoculture succeeds in post-traditional societies where identities are flexible commodities that have to adapt to consumption and constant change. In this respect, we think of ourselves as "free"—freed from tradition, free to choose who we want to be. On the surface this seems like a good thing—we are always told that the past is oppressive—but in practice the kinds of traditions that are eliminated by capitalist enclosure could also contribute to our well-being, helping us reconnect with our living systems. Eliminating traditional knowledge is a dangerous game, and though people in rich countries deride and expel immigrants based on a fantasy of cultural and racial purity, they depend on imported laborers that are still skilled in farming and ranching to maintain their food systems. Traditional knowledge also enables us to remain autonomous from the world system. Yes, we have the choice of being skaters, hip hoppers, ravers, or preppies, but increasingly many in the world don't have the luxury to shop for identities at the mall or on the internet. They are being displaced from the cultures, languages, and lands that have shaped their identities and are being forced into permanent migration. And media provide the selling points to justify this disruptive process.

Traditions are broken so that we become dependent on external forces for all our needs. In some cases laws are written and lives are brokered through trade agreements. In others we are seduced by cheap consumer goods. Eventually we are sucked into a kind of spiritual dependency in which the corporation, as evidenced in the Pepsi ad, becomes the mediator between us and the cosmos. The vision that advertising offers us is that we cannot understand ourselves or our place in the universe—or with nature for that matter—without the intervention and mediation of the world system. So though Shakira croons about the virtues of freedom, the system is designed to turn us into serfs.

(Re)Mediating Ecological Worldviews

A mixture of carbonated water and high fructose corn syrup sweetener produced through monocultural crop production, Pepsi is not just an innocuous soft drink: it's the world system in a disposable plastic container, a holon of a monocultural system of food production and consumption that includes genetically modified corn and its syrupy by-product. Pepsi is not in the business of traditional diets or healthy lifestyle choices. For many indigenous people, it's a recipe for diabetes. Soda is liquid candy, and typically Americans drink over fifty gallons of it a year.

Not to overstate the obvious, but by the time we consume products from companies like Pepsi, they are so far removed from their source of production that they might as well have been delivered by spacecraft (piloted by Shakira, of course). Like the smartphone, Pepsi's marketing image is pure, and whatever toxic by-products or health effects come from its production process and waste remain out of view to the average consumer. The Shakira ad, then, in fact propagates an ecological worldview, a mental model for how we engage (or not, as is most often the case) our living systems. As stated previously, all worldviews are environmental, because they determine how we act upon

Earth. Consequently, the world system is an expression of an ecological worldview, its economic orientation being a condition of how it believes the environment should be acted upon.

A Hierarchy of Needs

As stalkers and hunters of our attention, advertisers and marketers are scientists of human emotions. One way to understand how marketers and propagandists appeal to us on a primal level is by identifying our essential human needs. The psychologist Abraham Maslow developed a model of human motivation that looks like a pyramid. Starting at the base and moving up to the pyramid's apex, our needs are physiological (breathing, food, water, sex, sleep, homeostasis, excretion), safety (security of body, employment, resources, morality, family, health, property), love and belonging (family, friendship, sexual intimacy), esteem (self-esteem, confidence, achievement, respect of and by others), and self-actualization (morality, creativity, spontaneity, problem solving, lack of prejudice, acceptance of fact). This model is not infallible and can be critiqued from the perspective of ecopsychology (it lacks any mention of our need to connect with the natural world) or the yogic chakra system (it lacks a model of cosmology). Nonetheless, we can bounce off of Maslow to discuss how marketers hook our attention.

Media literacy activists argue that there are over thirty known "persuasion techniques." I prefer the term "attention-getting hook," because I believe that it better represents what they do. Essentially, a hook is a technique that grabs our awareness by working on us either emotionally or physiologically. The top three are sex, fear, and humor. These respectively draw on the first three levels of the pyramid of needs. Sex, of course, is a primary need for our species to procreate and experience deep intimacy, connection, and pleasure. Fear is what drives us to protect and secure ourselves. Humor is a form of connecting with others—jokes don't work unless we have shared understanding. It is a kind of inclusion. Once these emotions are generated, they are associated with the brand, a process called "emotional transfer."

For the average person, the cause of overconsumption is fairly obvious: to compensate for a lack of well-being, we shop. Some argue that our ancient brains are responsible. True enough. An innate need to hunt and gather gets translated from the ancient bush into the modern marketplace. Just as buying goods in the mall or through the shopping network gives people thrills, we also get small highs from purchasing gadgets and downloading apps to our smartphones. Additionally, a tendency to hoard and gorge comes from an unconscious fear that there may not be enough to eat tomorrow. To our primitive brains, starvation may be just beyond the horizon.

But these facts don't explain our overriding capacity to also moderate behavior, as difficult as it is for most of us to do. After all, cultural norms can change. Just look at the shift in attitude toward smoking over the past thirty years. There are plenty of examples of cultures that have balanced their biological needs with the spiritual and cultural well-being of their people. Through evolved cultural practices, they know not to overhunt and when conservation is an appropriate response to the limits of a given ecosystem. Throughout time, some cultures have succeeded while others have failed miserably at living within the parameters of their given ecosystems. However, unlike many ancient civilizations that did fail, an advantage we have is the knowledge of how past and current cultures have responded to their environments. It is fundamentally unethical that current colonial media practices deny the consequences of overshooting the carrying capacity of our living systems by masking this dangerous behavior with utopian images of growth and prosperity.

Whether people choose to attend to this knowledge is another matter. Media certainly play their part. Educationally, documentaries are excellent tools for conveying lessons from the past, though audiences for such fare are relatively small. By contrast, when the majority of media play up the growth and progress discourse above a conservation ethic, most people will identify with the hollow view that consumerism and technology can magically fix any problem, be it spiritual, cultural, or environmental.

If we are to transform ourselves toward a sustainable culture, then we need to take seriously the spiritual orientation of our society in which a sense of "lack" is filled by consumption. Overeating is a good example of how this plays out. Due to a convergence of politics, economics, and marketing, we have an overabundance of cheap calories in the daily American diet. This is why when you travel through the heartland of the United States you will get two plates of food whenever you order a meal at a restaurant or will be asked to "super size" at the fast food joint. A consequence is that obesity and diabetes have become endemic and normalized. But it's not just a matter of the system's shoveling food into our faces; many of us overeat because of spiritual malaise.

Sustainability is literally living within our means, whether it's maintaining a positive balance sheet in our checking accounts or with our carbon account in the atmosphere. Just as we cannot continue to live in debt, we also can't keep borrowing against the biosphere of the future. The reason we can consume at a rate of three Earths today is because we are bankrupting and impoverishing the future lives of our grandchildren and all their relations. The current moment calls for a sense of sufficiency that not only translates more broadly into our economics but, more importantly, becomes an integral aspect of our personal sense of well-being. The persistent theme of alienation, self-hatred, and fear of not fitting in propagated by marketing is designed to shatter our sense of wellness and autonomy in order to make us dependent on corporations to fulfill our psychological and spiritual needs. Sustainable media practice should uplift and educate in order to help us feel whole rather than fragmented.

It's time for marketing professionals to stop producing what ecoliteracy advocate Arran Stibbe identifies as "pseudo-satisfier," "dissatisfaction-manufacturing," and "convenience-constructing" discourses. In response to consumerism, we can advocate a steady state of contentment through connection (with people, places, ideas, animals, the cosmos), activity (physical, creative), curiosity (attention), learning, giving (volunteering, sharing), and understanding the difference between temporary and authentic happiness. Such would be the ultimate function of remediation: media as remedy.

TEK

Prior to the Spanish invasion, the diverse cultural landscapes of the Americas, including the Hopi, utilized traditional ecological knowledge (TEK). Many of these practices survive today because of the cultural commons. TEK proves to be very adaptable to local environments, because it's the product of thousands of years of research and development. For example, before the Spanish invasion and destruction of Tenochtitlan (now Mexico City), the Mexica's (Aztec) sophisticated mosaic of canals and terraced gardens were incredibly productive and efficient. In typical brute fashion, one of the first projects of Spanish engineers was to destroy these sophisticated gardens and replace them with their own system. The period of colonization was a systematic dismantling of bioregional food systems and agricultural practices in order to be replaced with those familiar to the Spanish: ranching, deforestation, and mining. However, not everything the

Spanish did was bad. Some of their best agricultural practices were adapted from North Africa, including dry-land farming techniques and irrigation, and the introduction of fruit and nut trees. In New Mexico the *acequia* irrigation system brought by the Spanish is one of the earliest post-contact forms of democracy and sustainable agricultural practice in North America. Nonetheless, colonization was a process of supplanting one energy system for another. Ultimately it was a horrific, net loss for pre-contact Americans.

Currently the dominant paradigm of globalization favors a third system, one based on techno-scientific agriculture, such as petroleum-based monocrops and genetically modified seed. However, this monocultural wave is contested by an opposite movement based on reviving traditional agricultural practices: permaculture, bioregionalism, farmers' markets, and slow food. These are a few examples of how the dominator complex is being challenged in people's daily practices. Alternative media play an important role helping these movements share and disseminate information. Through websites promoting open design (Open Source Ecology, http://opensourceecology.org), grassroots activism, books, and documentaries, the food movement gets its planetary legs through online networks. Such efforts are necessary to buttress the massive propaganda system at the disposal of the monocultural food system, as evidenced by the daily barrage of fast-food and junk-food marketing.

What's Your Feed?

The link between media and agriculture is not random. Many media related metaphors originally derive from food-growing practices: *culture* stems from the process of cultivation; *broadcast* comes from the act of seed casting; a signal's reception *field* corresponds with places that we grow things. Videos *stream* and we set up news *feeds*. Now we upload our data into *clouds* running in server *farms*. The precursor of the modern alphabet came from the record-keeping practices of farmers. Even the earliest DIY phone systems in the United States were strung through rural fences by ranchers who needed to communicate with each other.

But ultimately the link between food and media relates to the old saying, you are what you eat. We may use media to feed our minds with entertainment and information, but corporations also see us as food. The world system survives by consuming energy flows—material, mental, and spiritual. Our media habits require that we "spend" time, time being a currency of energy consumption and waste. The channeling of this energy is done via the medium of money. When corporations map the world—and by extension the business model for those media companies that serve the interests of the world system—the so-called bottom line is about determining who eats whose energy, and whose culture gets digested and whose doesn't.

Consider the primary financial model for the majority of media we use: advertising. The only way free media can make money is to sell your attention to advertisers.

If you don't watch or click, they don't make money. The inventory they are selling is our mental vitality, creativity, and interests. Subsequently, these media corporations and their advertisers are parasitic slime molds that can only thrive by harvesting the solar energy we collect from plant chemicals. Through the food we eat and the energy we expend, whenever we spend our money and time, these corporate entities gorge our stored solar energy. We work for them without pay.

The food system, like other institutional structures of the world system such as education or health care, reflects the mental models of the prevailing monocultural paradigm. To counter it we can repurpose the most ancient cultural knowledge we have—food—in order to foreground living systems into our thinking about a realm normally considered insulated from the natural world. In this sense, by tying media with food, we are remediating. *Remediation* is the technical term for restoring landscapes and habitats. It also has a health implication; in Spanish, *remedeos* are traditional herbal remedies. If we want to restore the balance of human affairs and living systems through our communication models, then we can borrow and reappropriate from the most essential activity of human culture: eating. Tied to eating are culture, economics, and ecology. It's no wonder that many of the world's leading proponents of sustainability see food as the primary access point for changing the world system. Indeed, as chaos theory argues, all systemic change is local. What is more local than the decision of what kind of food to put in your mouth? To extend that to media, we can also consider the implications of how we choose to feed our minds.

It's critical that we deal with interlocking colonial practices of the world system and its manipulation of media to shore up the existing system. For example, the average consumer is likely unaware that consolidated food empires—among the largest are Monsanto and Cargill—quietly monopolize planetary agricultural food systems with little to no discussion in the mainstream media. Inattention to these facts enables monocultural systems to maintain their hegemonic grip on the cultural commons and global trade policy. Moreover, we can see a parallel in how megacorporations like Monsanto use patenting as a form of colonial control and the manner in which media companies use copyright and the threat of piracy as a way of manipulating the cultural commons. Critically, alternative media in the form of documentaries and activist networks on the net educate and coordinate opposition to these powers.

Commercial Holons

We can think of the Pepsi ad as a boundary object, an artifact with commonly understood symbols but different levels of meaning depending on who comes into contact with it. Like a blueprint, it both describes and proscribes a worldview. As a boundary object, it has objective properties (thirty-second TV ad, featuring Shakira, etc.) but depending on who encounters it, its meaning and intention will vary. For example, Shakira and her management will view the ad as a vehicle for her career and part of developing her brand as an artist crossing over into the global market. The ad agency that produced it wants to make the most effective and powerful form of communication they can. Pepsi's shareholders want to see progress and growth in the Latin American market. Coca-Cola executives counter the campaign with their own message of unity and transformation. Univision ad sales executives are eager to sell the space for the ad. All these various intentions then come to fruition in the commercial, which becomes a microcosm of the whole system. It becomes a world system holon: a nodal expression within a complex network of power that reflects the system's properties like a knot in Indra's Net.

This is why advertisements are excellent objects to think about. As holons of the world system, despite their ubiquity, we barely notice them at all. Yet three thousand times a day, there they are comprising the greatest ambient myth-making machine in the history of the human race. They are so influential that we say they have no influence. But like pressing a tuning fork onto the body of a guitar, through media mindfulness we can apply our intelligence to get inside the mentality of the world system and grok its true essence. Such knowledge diminishes its power: it can only successfully operate under opaque conditions. It's like how insight meditation leads to understanding how our minds respond to our environment. Once we learn its secrets and tricks, its ability to continue business as usual becomes weakened. We break its spell.

Decolonizing Energy Systems

It has been argued that our modern economic paradigm derived from the co-evolution of communications technology and energy systems. In the modern age we have moved from the coupling of the printing press with the steam engine to radio/TV/satellite's interdependence with electricity. The rise of networked media intersects with the paradigm of distributed forms of renewable energy sources, because they both rely on decentralized systems. This evolutionary trajectory of media and energy coincides with systems theorist Ervin Laszlo's argument that our global system is transitioning from one based on conquest, colonization, and consumption to one motivated by connection, communication, and consciousness.

The world system at its core is biological and requires energy to run. Until now it has thrived in a relatively stable climate that has enabled a steady diet of nutrients and proteins to expand our species across the planet. The exponential growth of population in the past fifty years has a direct relationship with the consumption of cheap oil. But pirated solar energy in the form of oil comes with a price tag. We borrow against our children's future in order to compensate for overshooting our planet's current carrying capacity. Through advertising and the propagation of market ideology, media do their part by promoting the economic practices that enable the carbon economy.

Consequently the central energy paradigm of the past century, which is based on the carbon economy, has yet to give way to the kind of distributed systems inherent to communications based on the internet. The parallels are crucial. Fossil fuels depend heavily on centralized power and the national security state. Nuclear power, dependence on crude oil, and coal extraction require a massive industrial infrastructure and coordinated military operations. Such a convergence can be summarized by one of the Republican's leading demagogues, Newt Gingrich, who said, "You cannot put a gun rack in a Volt." Moreover, major corporate media stakeholders, such as GE and Westinghouse, emerged from the energy monopolies of the nineteenth century. Not surprisingly, the hegemonic model of mass media that emerges from such a system is co-dependent on the command and control paradigm: it reinforces the ideology that justifies resource wars (i.e., the Iraq War is never referred to as an "oil" war by the mainstream press) and media's economic model depends on ad revenue based on the carbon economy. Car manufacturers, for example, sponsor much of our media programming. Next time you watch TV, count the number of car or fossil fuel related services and products that are advertised. The internet is not immune. In fact, one of the scarier developments of the internet is the manner in which traditional energy companies have gamed the system so that their message is foregrounded in search engine requests for alternative energy and the environment or as contextual ads for sustainability themed news stories. Many news websites that feature environmentally themed stories have contextual ads that greenwash the major energy corporations of the world, such as Shell and Exxon.

The codependence between traditional mass media and the carbon economy can be seen in BP's response to the Deep Horizon oil spill in the Gulf of Mexico in 2010. By using chemical oil disbursements to eliminate the visual scourge of oil slicks, it was more an act of performative media than a cleanup operation. BP, likely in cooperation with the U.S. government, spun this event in ways that did not enable people to properly prepare for the consequences of what "really" happened to their local living systems. "Really" is put into quotes because the event had the opacity of oil itself through the censoring and blocking of the press from damaged ecosystems, and of course the strategic deployment of public relations. The use of the highly toxic Corexit 9500A to disperse ugly oil patches was like trying to use Photoshop to contain an oil spill, except far deadlier.

BP was also linked to a dubious website, the Deepwater Horizon Unified Command, which appeared to be an official clearinghouse for response information. Every day images on the site's splash page changed, but none of them had oil in them. One day it featured a turtle being cleaned, which was in stark contrast to a video elsewhere on the web that featured the testimony of a boat captain who claimed that turtles were being incinerated by BP's oil burn. Meanwhile, BP's PR people, masquerading themselves as journalists, reported from helicopters ridiculous statements like, "It's strangely peaceful up here—just right for surrendering to some meditation. . . . I'm filled with the wonderment of what's happening below our chopper only moments after it lifts off from an airport in Houma, Louisiana."

Recall that BP had already spent millions of dollars re-branding itself as "Beyond Petroleum," so managing the Gulf disaster became a kind of military-style disinformation campaign designed to control spin around the event so as to not tarnish its well-oiled public image. It appears to have been successful. The Gulf incident has disappeared from national discourse and business as usual seems to have gone on unabated. Oil drill permits and regulation proposals have given way to scare tactics of job loss and economic depression.

What the BP case shows is that media decolonization requires decoupling our media from the carbon economy. For those of us who use computers and networks, this will mean a transitional period, since currently our consumption of electronics and energy use are increasingly large sources of CO_2 emissions. In fact, computer networks now produce more carbon emissions than the airlines industry. A Google server farm will use as much electricity as a city of 250,000 people, so efforts by companies like Google to transition to renewable energy is absolutely necessary. But with the exponential growth of the information economy, we may be drowning in data anyway. For example, some communications scholars argue that data clouds, bloated software, redundant archiving, and media-rich data centers are pushing the overall planetary impact of physical data storage to unsustainable levels. ("The Internet Begins with Coal" titles one report about network power consumption.) They suggest that it will become increasingly necessary to ration data, meaning that people should be sharing copies of media rather than having to access them from multiple clouds. Unfortunately, the current push toward cloud computing by dominant corporate providers Balkanizes the net into data fiefdoms, leading to less compatibility and sharing. As long as we perpetuate the current fossil fuel regime, the belief that unlimited data is harmless to the biosphere will remain intrinsically bound to the creed that information is weightless and immaterial. This situation, the researchers argue, parallels our treatment of the oceans, which are being pushed to the brink of ecological collapse because people have assumed their capacity for producing food and absorbing pollution is limitless. Not only is linking computer and network usage directly to their impact on the environment a crucial step toward green cultural citizenship, it's a radical challenge to a status quo predicated on tightly restricted intellectual property. Proprietary control of data is the ultimate tragedy of the commons. Ultimately, only a culture based on a cultural commons that values sharing resources would ensure that the next wave of computing doesn't result in black clouds in our atmosphere.

We also need to rethink what we mean by *energy*. To reiterate, media driven by the colonial paradigm consume energy in the material sense, such as through physical transportation (books, magazines, DVDs, and media gadgets all have to be moved through space on boats, planes, trains, and trucks); resource use and waste (materials used to build sets for TV and film); power needed to operate media technology gadget production; and consumerism (product tie-ins, toys, clothing, etc. associated with big brands like Disney and Warner Bros.). All of these are tightly connected with a globalized system of distribution and production dependent on fossil fuels. But none of this is possible without the primary form of energy it needs to survive: our attention. Again, the world system is ultimately an energy parasite and thrives under two conditions. First is the general lack of awareness of its real nature. The magician is successful through diversion: we look at one hand while the illusion is carried out by the other. The second is that when our attention is transfixed in a channeled direction, our energy gets harvested. Our desires, interests, passions, survival instincts, and connectivity become "marketized" while our time gets "spent" to support a planet-destroying, consumptive lifestyle. Our attention is guided to ensure that we are dependent on the parasite, when ultimately the opposite is true: without us it cannot survive. Ultimately, the only entity that can directly address your consciousness is you. You are a key node in this system of relations. And as chaos theory argues, all systemic change is local. It is the everyday practices of ordinary people like us that ultimately perpetuate the system. So though a decolonized media means literally transitioning to alternative energy systems, the first step begins with our personal energy system in the form of attention.

Is it possible to create stories, engage in new cultural practices, and build appropriately scaled technology that no longer leaches the planet's finite resources and toxifies the biosphere? Ultimately the answer will come from our collective imagination. But to get started we can at least dispel the magic that interferes with our ability to see more clearly. Mapping the world system paradigm, looking at its evolution, and deconstructing its control strategies is part of the solution. Attention to our own dependency and inattention can help break previously existing cultural patterning. Social action and politics represents another level of response.

Ghost of Consciousness Past

Returning to the Shakira Pepsi ad, it is not without cosmic irony that she appears with a crucifix. The version of globalization offered by Pepsi extends the mentality of the cross critiqued by the Hopi. Yet maybe we also see hints of something emerging, as if a ghost in the machine is reaching out to us. In the ad a circle in the shape of the spherical Pepsi logo accompanies the cross. But they are still separate. While it's certainly true that the form of globalization transferring control from the Church to the corporatocracy is undesirable, let's suppose for a moment that the world system is gestating the symbolic zeitgeist to give birth to something new, that the various humans making media have some innate connection to Earth reaching through them.

It would be a "success" of hegemony if we could no longer imagine anything outside or beyond it. Seeing transglobal capitalism as transient and impermanent is a necessary step to dissolve its spell. Moreover, concerts and church gatherings can be positive ritual spaces. Art and music have the power to heal and disseminate ideas. In a postcolonial mediasphere, these kinds of encounters happen simultaneously as local and planetary experiences. By removing Pepsi and Shakira from the equation, we reoccupy these ritual spaces. We also have a template for successful storytelling. The world system can tell effective stories, but cues exist within its dreaming mind indicating an Earth consciousness is waiting to be born among its planetary inhabitants.

CHAPTER 4

Evolving Media Ecosystems

Just as the abuse victim may have out-of-body experiences as a way of dealing with trauma, ecopsychologists argue the repressed pain of severing an intimate relationship with our natural landscapes has led to increased disembodiment writ large. The thing that can turn us into aliens is the distance we maintain from an embodied connection with Earth through projecting our consciousness into the mediasphere. One strategy is to displace trauma through our media by allowing them to capture our voices and essence. And when we feel that loss, we ask media to recycle it back to us through greater stimulation. Hence films, commercials, and TV become increasingly violent and sexualized—because we want to feel ourselves.

The history of media makes this point more clearly. Marshall McLuhan argues that we extend our senses into media. The phone extends the ear and voice. The telescope and microscope expand our vision. But when we enlarge ourselves externally, we simultaneously numb ourselves locally. We "autoamputate" our senses as we turn them over to media technologies. A simple example is that we unlearn math when we use calculators. A more complicated one is when some become dependent on porn for sexual intimacy instead of relying on human contact. Or how horror films are popular because they jar our senses. Remember that all media start as nerve stimulation. Our thought forms are afterimages of the direct stimulus of light photons and sound waves that come into contact with our bodies.

As a result we are physically manipulated by a "creeping cycle of desensitization." This means that as media technologies evolve, they normalize and plateau certain levels of nerve stimulus. And since the economy of attention dictates that the way to rise above the clutter is to out-stimulate the competition, we are repeatedly exposed to greater levels of sex, violence, and audio-visual shock. Go to YouTube and compare an early James Bond trailer such as *Dr. No* with a contemporary version, like *Quantum of Solace.* You will be amazed by how painfully slow the old one feels. Additionally, notice how TV news has become a roller coaster of colors and sound effects designed to raise your blood pressure, or how newscasters focus on conflict rather than resolution. The intent is to make you feel very unsettled.

It's no wonder school kids are so agitated: the ancient, reptilian parts of their brains are being jostled by fast edits and juxtapositions at increasingly faster rates. In response, of course, the world system offers parents and teachers a cure through medication. Attention deficit hyperactivity disorder is seen as pathology, as opposed to a sensible response to a disturbed society. It's a vicious cycle: our attention is sold to the highest bidder; we get bored with the status quo, so we crave higher levels of stimulation; we drug ourselves to stabilize; then the stimulation is amped up even more. It's classic addictive behavior.

Brain Ecosystems

Writing is very much a "seeing" kind of activity. It's very surgical, a kind of focused vision necessary for hunting that is transferred to the pen. In a literate society, magic shifts from the landscape to the word. First, consider how paper is reconstituted organic matter (with a smattering of chemicals). When we read on paper the clusters of symbols we call words, images appear in our minds. This kind of activity is familiar to us, so it doesn't seem at all strange to make this point. But when literate folks first encountered non-literate peoples and saw them communicating with animals, plants, trees, and minerals, they called them uncivilized and crazy. But they just learned to "read" differently than we did! We need satellites to predict the weather, but land-based peoples can observe ants or listen to owls to know when and how the weather will change.

Literate cultures are inherently schizophrenic because they tend to be mentally unbalanced. This is why you should be cautious when people hastily anticipate the global networked mind or the singularity: just because our media create a planetary brain doesn't mean it's a sane one. The problem is emphasizing one kind of sense experience over others. Consider our basic words for sight and sound. We hear and listen; we watch and see. Hearing and watching are mainly right-brain activities: they involve taking in fields of sensory experience and are part of our pattern-seeking capacity. They are necessary for understanding changes in the environment, and hence our survival. We take in our surroundings, model them, and watch for changes. When the *gestalt* of our surroundings is altered significantly (such as by the stampede of elephants or jumping lions), we can respond appropriately. That's where listening and seeing become necessary. We focus our attention in order to respond appropriately to the details of our environment. The brain then synthesizes the sensory experience to ask "what if" questions in order focus our energy on the proper solution (such as aiming a spear to kill a predator or running away).

Is it possible that sustainable behavior comes from cultivating right-brain thinking? Psychiatrist Iain McGilchrist points out that the right brain's job is to inhibit immediate responses to situations so that we can use our wit and empathy to work out solutions. It also helps map and simplify the world so that we can make better sense of it. Metaphor, implicit meaning, body language, embodied experience, and a disposition for living rather than mechanical reality characterize the right-brain approach to the world.

The machine model is self-consistent because it made itself that way. It's what he calls the "Berlusconi of the brain" (named after the media mogul who is the former prime minister of Italy) because it controls all the "media"—the right hemisphere doesn't have a voice. The left brain model of the world is like a hall of mirrors, a reality bubble. McGilchrist argues that the left hemisphere is a closed system that demands perfection, whereas the right hemisphere's understanding of the world is an open system. In the end, it's not reason versus imagination; you can't have one without the other. The problem with our current world system is that it's based on a closed, machine-like model of the world built by an unbalanced, and ultimately, insane mind. To restore sanity, we need to rebalance how we perceive the world and ourselves.

The left and right hemispheres work well together: they are a team. Treated separately, one tends to not like the other. Consider how artists and scientists often view each other, but also what happens when they work together. The Hopi speak of the difference between the right and left side of the body, and how the right side (controlled by the left hemisphere) is the seat of "evil" because it is not where the heart resides. But we should be weary of projecting duality on the Hopi understanding of our bodies: it's not one versus the other, but a matter of the hemispheres not working in balance with each other.

The intriguing possibility is that sustainable behavior comes from cultivating right-brain thinking. Media emerging from participatory culture appear to be more balanced in terms of combining text and images, and hence more balancing for the brain hemispheres. This may be why so many traditional intellectuals accuse the internet of making us "stupid." Old-school modernists appear nostalgic for the solitude and individualized deep thought that comes with print culture. Media alone, of course, should not be considered proper therapy for the cognitive disjuncture we experience with such rapidly changing technologies. Rather, we should heed the Greeks and Buddhists and remember that moderation and media fasting is also necessary.

The Consumer Sublime

The rise of industrialization in the eighteenth and nineteenth centuries produced a countermovement, the progenitors of modern environmentalism, Romanticism. The Romantics began to differentiate between urban civilization and "nature." They railed against the destructive turn of civilization and urbanization, and began to revere the "natural sublime," the sense of awe that we experience when we cannot contain the phenomenon of nature within rational thought. The most famous work that depicts this perspective is Caspar David Friedrich's 1818 painting "Wanderer above the Sea of Fog." Here a silhouetted "man of means" stares from a rock precipice into an abyss filled with craggy rocks and fog. He is an educated urbanite who has become a spectator of nature.

Again, trying to make the familiar strange, this concept that cities and nature are different realities is a very new idea. As unintegrated modern folk, we don't remember or know what it's like to have our lives integrated intimately with the landscape. We are brought up and trained to see difference. Consider the typical SUV spot on TV. "Nature" is not where humans live. Rather it is an unspoiled and pure playground where work doesn't take place. As the mediator between the human world and "nature," the SUV becomes our spaceship to that place. It's a world system portal to the sublime.

Even the idea of "nature as sublime" is modern, for it implies a rare, unfamiliar experience in nature. In the 1800s when cities, trains, and industrialization deadened the senses and quickened time, poets and painters went to the country to reconnect with a natural "other." The works of Thoreau and Emerson are the legacy of that trip. But not to be outdone by nature, which was "out there," during the Industrial Revolution human inventiveness started to capture that sense of sublime again. The earliest bridges, skyscrapers, and power plants had this effect. The Niagara Falls power plant and Brooklyn Bridge were huge attractions that instilled a sense of awe for the people who flocked to see these new marvels of human inventiveness. Over time the "sublime" has become something to be consumed, and like the creeping cycle of desensitization, the bar keeps getting raised. This is particularly evident in media spectacle.

Through its sublime attractions, the world system uses technology as a kind of self-justification. The sense of awe it creates within us means that it must be an important, legitimate force on Earth worthy of worship. But is there really such a clear boundary between the natural and consumer sublime? Let's compare the experience of going into the Grand Canyon versus watching an IMAX movie on the canyon's edge (yes, it's possible). The IMAX website promises that its moving image technology enables you to "hear more, see more." At the Grand Canyon IMAX you can see naturalist Wade Davis of *National Geographic* featured in the documentary, *Grand Canyon: River at Risk.* On the one hand it seems absurd to watch this film inside a dark theater on the Grand Canyon's rim when you could simply hike down and have the experience yourself. On the other hand, not everyone can travel there (the film can be seen in other theaters) and it does create an intimate experience that technology enables (such as telescopes or microscopes enhancing the invisible).

This contradiction is similar to that which German philosopher Walter Benjamin grappled with. He argued that although art loses its "aura" when reproduced, it also becomes democratized because it is available to everyone. The danger is when the technological sublime services fascism and war, as was the case with the Nazis. And isn't the Iraq War's "shock and awe" campaign the ultimate world system sublime? Because of film, war becomes a spectacle for audiences to enjoy—never mind what it's like for the people at the receiving end of bombing campaigns. Politics by aerial bombardment and drone strikes is a logical extension of the outsourcing and distancing that technology enables, and by becoming a means of entertainment, it is yet another way to eschew responsibility for our actions.

Any new medium both enhances and eliminates some sensory experience—no doubt certain aspects of nature become accessible to us through film and TV, while others are inadvertently cut off. BBC's *Planet Earth* series, for example, takes us places we can never go, or allows us to see animals we'll never know intimately. *Winged Migration* can show us a bird's worldview in a way that we may never know (unless we become a shaman, that is). Suffice to say, to some the natural sublime can be present in some kinds of media. The danger of spectacularizing nature is that it can be devoid of politics. Can we legitimately celebrate animals and "unspoiled" habitats in the absence of a serious discussion of the world system's ecocidal policies? Is it ethical for nature film productions to accept sponsorship from companies that use such material to greenwash their toxic operations?

Because of our addiction to speed and thrills, in the future people may only seek experiences of awe through those generated via media and theme parks. In the process of hyper-stimulation we numb ourselves to the subtle voices of the extended world of living systems. Our ability to listen to the animals, plants, and mountains is diminished because with our technologically mediated sublime, we cease to be *here*. Just like the old phone ad that promised we can "be there now," many of us are losing our minds to that distant horizon line while simultaneously neglecting our bodies and the Earth that nurtures us.

Empathy

Languages evolve collectively. Languages—or more accurately, linguacultures—are reality ecologies. So are media. Different media have ecologies of perception bias, such as toward time or space. For example, oral culture requires your presence in time. Unless you are there to hear it, you will not know it. Many oral cultures distinguish between those kinds of knowledge that are based on direct experience versus those that are known through second-hand experience (such as knowing about something only from stories). Most languages until very recently, say the last few hundred years, were embedded in place. The proliferation of English as an international language as embedded in trade and media demonstrates the extent to which globalized culture has moved further away from its place-based roots.

In our high-tech metropolitan reality, much of what we know is secondary experience. We don't really understand most of the things we claim to "know." It's not necessarily false knowledge, but rather it is the illusion of immediacy. It's important to be aware of the difference and to not be fooled into thinking that just because we see a video or photo of something we truly understand it, or that it represents something "real." We are conditioned to believe that media embody the essence of things, but mostly they just re-present them through various mechanisms of framing and filtering.

On the other hand, media perform a vital function: empathy. They don't just extend us physiologically, but emotionally as well. Though I have been emphasizing the negative character of most world system media, the extension of our senses to parts of the world where there have been disasters, revolution, and war has very powerfully enabled us to cultivate new awarenesses and true feelings of solidarity. The importance of empathy isn't trivial. Let's compare two conflicts from two different eras of media: the Spanish Civil War of the 1936–39 and the Egyptian uprising that marked the Arab Spring of 2011.

I'm loath to make historical analogies, simply because every historical moment has its own unique characteristics that would not be possible if we impose nonexistent conditions. So as the clutch mechanism of time slips, it would be unfair to compare the moment of democratic potential in the Arab world with those events in Spain when the libertines of Catalunya battled Franco's fascist forces. Unlike the revolutionary contagion that is transforming the Mediterranean and beyond, for the Republicans of Spain, history didn't side with them. The freedom fighters of the Spanish Civil War were crushed and wiped out as the world's leaders stood by, or as was the case of Stalin and Hitler, made sure that they were destroyed.

So how does the Spanish Civil War connect with our current planetary fight for democracy? During the Egyptian uprising of 2011 (and then subsequently Bahrain, Yemen, Libya, and Syria), I monitored via the Twitterverse the incredible ways in which everyday Egyptians self-organized to fill the space of a collapsed state. I was reminded of George Orwell's profound passages in *Homage to Catalonia* about a free Barcelona during the early days of the Spanish Civil War. In it he describes a spirit of cooperation and brother/sisterhood that permeated cafés and barber shops alike, one in which a temporary autonomous zone of human potential was freed from the restraints of state terror and mechanized control. To behold such a space is a beautiful thing. To live it is a miracle. To unlearn it is impossible.

Now, one thing (among many, which makes this just a thought exercise) that differentiates the current situation from Spain in 1936 is the global interconnectedness of the events unfolding on our screens. Though the Republicans defending against Franco were shored up by a vast solidarity movement from around the world that sent volunteers and fighters to aid their embattled democracy, few could monitor and mobilize support in real time to prevent the horror that was unleashed by Franco and his allies. Consider the amount of time it took for Orwell to write down and publish his thoughts versus the speed by which ideas move around the globe today. Just as importantly, jet travel enables veterans of the Arab revolutions to travel around the world to assist their planetary compatriots. During the Egyptian uprising my own particular formula for monitoring events was a combination of Al Jazeera English's live internet stream, the UK *Guardian*'s live news blog, Twitter, and *Mother Jones*'s "explainer" page. From these primary portals, three of which are traditional news organizations that have evolved to incorporate the net, I could link into a variety of new sources. In particular I diversified my Twitter stream to be more inclusive of non-Western perspectives. Compared to the universe of American corporate power, this was really a whole different reality.

Though I wasn't on the ground in Egypt to provide any physical assistance, through the internet I could track, share, connect, and extend an invaluable resource that drives any revolution: empathy. To invoke something as woo-woo as "empathy" seems rather weak in comparison to the kinds of assistance that foreign brigadistas gave the Spanish Republicans. But solidarity is a powerful force that feeds the people engaged in real struggle. The worst feeling is to be in an isolated cell somewhere, subject to random torture, knowing that you are completely alone and without help, as was the case for Spanish libertines who were abandoned after the fall of their republic. People are biologically wired for connection and thrive from positive feedback. No wonder, then, that the Arab Spring and its sibling movement, Occupy, have disseminated globally. It's not just a result of mediating information, but resonance.

Aside from supporting political struggles, media can offer other deep emotional resonances with planetary consciousness. An example from pop culture can be seen in the film *Love Actually*. Unlike typical Hollywood fare that's driven by spectacles of violence, the film's opening and closing scenes focus on the normal, daily occurrence of communion and compassion experienced by loved ones reuniting at an airport terminal. These scenes emphasize the sense of pleasure and love we experience when coming home. Imagine if such feelings could be extended to Earth, so that we begin to reconnect with our planet as home in the same way we do with our immediate families and inhabited landscapes. Documentaries about endangered species, the plight of the planet, and nature films can do just that. Though these should not be considered as substitutes for genuine bonding experiences with living systems, they offer pathways to connection, understanding, and empathy. As the film theorist Sean Cubitt argues, if we do not know, we will not care. For many, media technology will be their gateway to ecological awareness.

As an example of empathic media from the realm of participatory culture, YouTube curated an experimental documentary in which users were asked to submit videos about one day in their lives, July 24, 2010. The resulting film, *Life in a Day,* offers a wonderful glimpse into the lives of ordinary people across the planet. One is left with a strong feeling of love that eschews the normal negativity associated with films dealing with the human condition. In another experiment that connects disparate expressions of humanity, a DJ named Kutiman created the "Thru-you" project (http://thru-you.com). Taking advantage of the plethora of YouTube videos uploaded by musicians showing off their chops, he collected various unrelated clips to remix them into new songs and then uploaded them back to YouTube. One of this project's videos, "I M New," magically blends these initially disconnected artists, producing a synchronistic mix of emergent cultural expression. The unpredictable result of these unexpected collaborations is exactly the stuff of evolution: mutation. Here a hardy mix of empathy, creativity, recombination, collaboration, and play—the core of music's timeless appeal as a laboratory of cultural experimentation—represents key ingredients for cultural transformation. Again, on a planetary scale open networks enable the kind of sharing that makes cultural evolution possible, but without an ethic of care driven by compassion, there will be little chance of solving our planetary crisis. People will only save that which they care about. Empathy, then, becomes a powerful weapon against the abstractions that make exploitation palatable.

The Global Brain

When it comes to connecting living systems with media, we have a big blind spot. This blind spot is both intentional and unconscious. Many gadget manufacturers, for example, would prefer not to expose their supply chain to the scrutiny of environmental or social justice activists. A lack of interest upon the average consumer to know this information is probably less deliberate because these issues aren't even on his or her radar. Indeed, as activists trying to save the commons have argued, it's difficult to salvage something that few people even know exists. In an era when the "ownership society" and privatization is gospel, it's certainly not in the interest of corporate media to advertise or promote the existence of the commons. If it is not discussed or represented, it doesn't exist.

Likewise, arriving at an understanding of how our personal media ecosystems are connected to living systems won't come easily to people heavily conditioned by our system to believe that Western cultural values and technology are the result of social Darwinism. Such a belief is a legacy of colonialism, which for ideological reasons applied the insights of evolutionary biology to cultural realities as a way of justifying exploitation. If indigenous peoples were considered inferior and not technologically advanced, then it was for their own good that Western powers colonized their resources and destroyed their cultures in order to advance them. Even Marx advocated the colonization of India in order to help create an industrial proletariat. This rhetoric has its parallel in some versions of technological determinism that see the rise of global networks as the beginning stage of creating a global brain. The rhetoric of an interconnected nervous system facilitated by computer networks sounds appealing, yet it is potentially dangerous if we don't consider the implications of building a distorted and alienated brain. The history of media technology is a mixed bag of liberating potential and increasing alienation that has served some cultural interests and hurt others. The slew of books that have come out to cheer on the rise of social media as a liberating game changer have yet to bring their arguments to the majority of populations of the world who are dealing with the environmental and social impact of our consumption patterns and media habits.

Many well-meaning activists promote computing as an aspect of natural human evolution without regard to the fact that technologies come about as the result of choice and are not bequeathed by supernatural powers. Unless, that is, you want to call the market's "invisible hand" such a force. For example, MIT's Nicholas Negroponte has devised the One Laptop Per Child (OLPC) program as a means of lifting underserved communities across the globe out of poverty. In theory if children in poor countries are given durable, cheap computers with internet access, they will enter the global economy to improve the condition of their families and communities. But an online commercial promoting the program embeds some dubious cultural assumptions. The ad features an African man (his country of origin is not clear) in traditional dashiki trying to predict rainfall. When he fails to forecast the weather, his neighbors mock him, and he returns home embarrassed. Upon seeing his distraught father, his son pulls out an OLPC that has access to a satellite weather service. Armed with correct scientific knowledge, the man succeeds to impress his neighbors with a newfound ability to prophesy. The ad suggests that our protagonist is not worthy of his family or community until he adapts Western ways of knowing. Through its caricature of "primitive" Africans, it disregards the importance of local knowledge of the environment. This is not to say that disadvantaged Africans should not have access to the same opportunities as those in the West who have the privilege of using advanced technology. But technology disembedded from local realities ultimately won't solve the deeper problems of our system.

Maybe we should look to African traditions for inspiration rather than assuming that cheap computers based on Western cultural assumptions will solve all their problems. In fact, Ubuntu, the name of the open source Linux operating system, comes from the Bantu (southern African) philosophy meaning, "I am what I am because of who we all are." To Negroponte's credit, the OLPC was designed as open source and therefore sharable. Accordingly, net optimists like Charles Leadbeater believe the emerging character of the web can be summed up as, "you are what you share," something much closer to most indigenous belief systems than the mentality at the root of our modern system based on the idea of individualism. So though technological evolution has veered toward reinforcing the Industrial paradigm of hierarchical control, perhaps some innate characteristics of human evolution have drawn us toward a sharable and participatory reality.

Nonetheless, before we cheer on the growth of an impending global brain, it's imperative that we reflect more honestly on the more alienating aspects of our media ecosystem's evolution. Otherwise we threaten to do more harm than good. Many media technologies serve as platforms for tremendous creativity, which can cause some people to take personally the ecological critique at hand. Rather than go into denial, we can remain optimistic for the prospects of an evolving, global nervous system based on empathy and resonance; rather than perpetuate the monocultural reduction of the world into a marketplace, any global brain should ultimately be connected to the planetary heart.

CHAPTER 5

Gardening Media Ecosystems

The contact point between the world system and the planetary heart can be found in the zone of human experience. Such a space is transitional and can be understood by looking at it as a kind of ecotone. *Ecotone* is the landscape ecology term for an edge environment, or zone between ecological systems, such as the area between a forest and meadow. This dynamic border region has aspects of the differing zones, but is itself unique. Changes in the ecotone's structure are caused by disturbances. In many cases such changes will impact the ecotone without significantly altering the core ecologies that border it. So let's assume that a person functions within a personal media ecotone—a kind of information ecology that comprises people, institutions, communication devices, and cultural beliefs. This complex ecology interfaces with the world system and anima mundi, but on different scales depending on many factors. For example, marketers often speak of social networks and gadgets as different media "ecosystems," such as the Facebook or iPhone ecosystem. There is some truth to these claims if we take the word *ecosystem* to mean a "system of systems." True enough, Facebook has its own ecology, as do Twitter and Google. Enter into any of these portals and you'll experience a network of connections and relations that are conditioned by the rules and connections afforded by that particular system. Nonetheless, these metaphors are ultimately incomplete and false because they lack a connection or awareness of how these media ecosystems are connected to living systems—cultural and biological. Bringing living systems back into media ecosystems requires a shift in perspective.

Though I'm reluctant to make all ecological concepts analogous to media (for example, I don't think an information meme is the same as cell DNA), I do think from an Earth Democracy perspective, the concept of a biome is incredibly useful. Biomes are large ecosystem habitats such as steppes, grasslands, and savannas. If media are cognitive environments that we inhabit (and hence rely on to shape our perspectives regarding the natural world), then being conscious of the mental (or "built") biome of a mediasphere is vital for becoming mindful of our beliefs regarding the physical ecology we inhabit. We can amplify this argument to say perception is also technologically influenced, with media being primary agents in not only transmitting ideas between people, but also actually producing worldviews.

If each biome is governed by energy flow, then in a mediasphere there are two kinds of energy consumption: the first is the energy necessary to power and create the media biome (such as electricity or petroleum to make consumer electronics or power the internet); the second is the cognitive energy necessary to process the media, and the biopower that makes media possible. As argued previously, corporate media are powered by advertising, which is necessary to garner our attention so we will buy products; buying products means spending money; money is made through work—our individual labor or biopower. A media biome fueled by corporations is going to have different implications than those composed of nonprofits or local communities. They have different energy and metabolic needs. Community media will require fewer biopower resources for both production and consumption because they do not require advertising.

Biomes are connected by organisms. Corporations are a kind of built organism, as is a city and other human communities. People are also information organisms that move between media biomes, immigration being an important way information is exchanged between zones. Applied to cognition, how we treat the environment is analogous to how we treat the mind. The mind that categorizes a forest as an industrial resource will likewise design education to produce industrial minds. If we view the mind as an organic garden, then forests will be engaged differently. If we view media as a collective space for cognitive gardens to flourish, this departs substantially from the view that the cultural commons is a resource to be exploited and commodified.

Media Ecotones

Each media ecotone is a distinct environment, and since we have bodies that move through space and extend into other spaces, such as those mediated by technology, then our personal environments vary considerably and are often transitional. Moreover, we don't just move through the environment as separate entities, as is the case in a mechanistic reality construct, but *through a world* of affordances that lead to shifting subjectivities. For example, a person navigating a new city such as Rome without a map will have an entirely different experience than the person who uses a smartphone with various apps that augment the cityscape according to its software and geolocation functions. Thus, the kinds of devices and media that we interact with will produce different relationships with the world.

The media ecotone comprises a mix of practices, social relationships, values, and technology uses in the specific reality of the media practitioner. This nuanced understanding of technology enables an empowered stance in which media technology's influence is not autonomous from user interactions with it, as anti-technologists like to argue, but guided by personal practice. What makes technology appear autonomous is when its users behave as mere consumers without actively engaging their media systems as green cultural citizens.

The border region of a media ecotone is a space of transformation, one that's rich and diverse. In order to be deepened by the ecotone, however, we have to become media ecologists. An ecologist is one who perceives the system's pattern and mediates like a gardener intervenes in a garden: she works with the various materials and properties available to the system and then channels the necessary resources so that it can thrive, not just for the current moment, but also for the future.

But how do we garden this convoluted and distorted mediasphere that we navigate on a daily basis? The world system reproduces itself in the mundane daily practices of everyday life. We come into contact with the system continually. Media practice varies, but it is the one thing you do have control over, albeit options are limited according to what the system affords. For example, not everyone is a DIY media maker or hacker. Some people just want simple communication devices and entertainment that doesn't require tweaking or critical thought. Others like to tinker. An iPhone or Android phone allows different possibilities, just as open system internet browsers like Mozilla's Firefox have different user experiences than closed system browsers like Microsoft's Explorer. Regardless of your preference, without attending to the possibilities afforded by our dependence on media devices and how we engage the mediasphere—without a green perspective—the corporatocracy will colonize it without regards to its impact on living systems.

Media Are a Disturbance

Media are not monolithic, nor are humans programmable machines. We are biological creatures that learn from environments in the same way that children acquire language. Instead of calculators with buttons to be pushed, the brain is more like a garden. A garden is cultivated not just individually but within a context of tradition and experience; hence the term *culture* reflects how our beliefs are grown and nurtured. Initially *culture* referred to the domestication of plants, as in *agriculture*. In the 1800s it took on the connotation of something that is learned, in particular for those that had the privilege of elite education or social status. Thus in many contexts high culture is associated with museums, opera, symphonies, and classical traditions of European culture. More generically *culture* has come to mean shared meaning that comes through social learning. Ultimately, as the poet and deep ecologist Gary Snyder remarks, "'She's cultured' shouldn't mean elite, but more like 'well-fertilized.'"

Unless confined to a highly controlled greenhouse environment, gardens are open systems. But even an industrial greenhouse, such as those that grow hot house tomatoes, requires high inputs, such as water and energy, not to mention the materials and resources necessary to create the structures. Outdoor gardens are not confined to the specific space they occupy but are also part of extended systems that include regional weather, geological soil conditions, human laws, regional water rights, and so on. Hence, gardens are sites of cultural intervention and interaction with living systems.

Many have taken up the idea that media should be viewed from the perspective of "media environmentalism." Media scholar George Gerbner calls for a "culture environment movement," essayist Susan Sontag argues that we need an "ecology of images," intellectual property scholar

James Boyle promotes "information environmentalism," and Marshal McLuhan inspired the notion of "media ecology." All of these suggest an approach that media are akin to commonly shared natural environments, such as preserves or parks. Unfortunately, none of these writers have dealt with media and their connection with living systems, but only draw upon the metaphor of ecology to argue for wiser policies toward the public sphere or moderating technology. So what happens if this metaphor is taken literally, if media were indeed a kind of living system? From this perspective, much can be learned from ecological sciences.

When a new element disturbs an ecosystem's "equilibrium," such as an invasive species, it becomes a different ecosystem. That process is called succession. The notion of equilibrium has to be in quotation marks because plant ecologists no longer see ecosystems as stable or balanced but in constant change. The changes oscillate within perimeters that appear to be stable during given time frames, but the view of nature as eternally balanced is more a projection of human desire over the reality at hand. Likewise, Buddhists and brain scientists acknowledge that mind states are highly unstable and shift constantly. The appearance of a unified and stable self is an amazing construct of consciousness that enables us to survive, but when scrutinized more closely it is in fact an illusion. Gardening and meditation, then, have similarities in that they require careful observation and experimentation to test what does and doesn't work for particular environments, be they landscapes, culturescapes, mindscapes, or mediascapes. In essence, we should become media gardeners.

The level of change to the system depends on its resilience. Some systems, especially those that are full of diversity, can handle great disturbances, which gives them economies of flexibility. Hurricanes, for example, have less impact on communities surrounded by biotic buffer zones with rooted plant life that has evolved to withstand the disturbance of high-powered winds. Tradition is another important aspect of resiliency. In Japan, in order to help people survive tsunamis there are ancient stone markers that instruct inhabitants to not build below certain elevation points. Had modern developers been in touch with this traditional knowledge, the scale of disaster of the earthquake-caused tsunami in 2011 would have been lessened. As diversity is eliminated—biological and cultural—systems become less resilient. Human languages—and hence entire systems of knowledge, perception, and survival strategies—are getting wiped out in the name of progress.

Systems theorists argue that every system is based on mental models that are internally consistent. They get the results they are designed to get, but at the same time they tend to ignore knowledge or information that is inconsistent with their reality models. As long as there is reinforcing ("positive") feedback, its proponents will believe the system is a success. This is called the snowball effect, because as a closed system the snowball grows and expands through reinforcing feedback. It does what it's supposed to do, but at the expense of the environment it's working in. Balancing ("negative") feedback ensures the healthy functioning of systems. Our brains, for example, have inhibiters that keep our neurons from firing into exponential epileptic fits. At a tribal level, cultures with appropriate taboos against over-consumptive behavior serve as a balancing mechanism against exploitation of environmental resources. In Europe, up until the Renaissance, due to a general belief in anima mundi there was a strong ethic of restraint against the overexploitation of nature. The emergence of the Industrial-Scientific Revolution changed our cultural ethical framework, enabling corporations to become what they are today.

When pundits or marketers uncritically promote the ideology of growth, they inadvertently reinforce the most detrimental and unsustainable aspect of current media: they continue to give the false (and dangerous) impression that business as usual can be maintained at its current level. One way that media could introduce balancing feedback into our cultural system is to function like those speed monitors we see on highways. They reflect back to us our velocity so that we can make appropriate adjustments to stay within the accepted limits of the system. Another kind of balancing feedback is empathy, which limits or inhibits exploitative cultural practices.

The world system prevails when we don't attend to its primary disturbance mechanism: advertising. Again, we inhabit cognitive and cultural landscapes that offer us cues for how to function in the world. In some cases marketing works very well, in others not at all. In Iran, for example, beginning in the 1950s part of the modernization strategy instituted by the Shah (with the backing of the CIA and U.S. aid) was to promote Western ideology through TV. But Western images combined with a ruthless police state produced the opposite effect: in 1979 Iran experienced a revolution that led to the formation of the currant Islamist government. It was in fact alternative media, in the form of a distributed network of audiocassettes, that enabled the opposition to spread its message and subvert the state's propaganda system. In other parts of the world, however, media and American inspired pop culture have helped spread the myths of the commodities system, making modernity sexy and desirable. Such is the strategy when Pepsi uses Shakira to hawk its brand around the world. The results it produces are hard to measure. Some viewers are more vulnerable than others. The kinds of things that make a difference are education, strong social ties, loving families, resilient communities, strong cultural traditions, and healthy self-esteem. Not everyone exposed to advertising is going to convert to the world system cult. But ads do shape our collective imagination. They shape associations and rearrange symbolic relationships. Those effects are immeasurable, but you can be sure that the millions of dollars spent on marketing are not spent for the heck of it. Money is spent for behavior modification and there is a belief on the part of the creators that it works. An important point of resistance, then, is to destabilize the power of these symbolic associations.

Another example of media disturbance is terrorism, in particular the example of 9/11. The event of the Twin

Towers cannot be thought of outside the context of TV. It was an image event staged for the global mediasphere. Regardless of who instigated it, the event caused an immediate and global reaction with consequences that are still felt today, yet how people responded to it reflects their particular media ecotones. From one perspective, people said it changed everything. From another, it just reinforced and made stronger particular tendencies within the system (for example, it provoked the military establishment to get even more entrenched in a combative framework against the world). What is more important from the perspective of media disturbance is how it reverberated as a tool of propaganda. It created an easily digested symbolic cluster that politicians could use to justify wars and the subversion of civil liberties. Corporate media uncritically accepted the government's narrative of the event. Independent media makers and journalists produced documentaries and investigative journalism that challenged government propaganda, and on the internet there was a veritable cottage industry of documentaries, discussion boards, and video channels promoting dozens of conspiracy theories about the nature of the event.

Ultimately, media disturbances take on different forms but have in common the character of being novel and eventful. They can be staged guerilla tactics waged by groups like Greenpeace, mediated environmental disasters like BP's Deep Horizon catastrophe, public relations stunts by corporations, natural calamities like Hurricane Katrina, activist videos documenting police abuse, sleuths uploading politician gaffs to YouTube, or pop culture that taps into the zeitgeist. How these particular disturbances play out depends on human diversity, network resiliency, cultural niches, symbolic watersheds, and mediaspheric biomes.

Avatar's Mediasphere Disturbance

Most media activist strategies are based on a mechanistic view of the mind. When the mind is viewed as a machine, social and cultural problems are approached as matters of programming: get people the right kind of information and they will make rational choices. This "information deficit model" underlies the belief that good journalism and unbiased information are the key to a better informed citizenry. But psychologists—and marketers for that matter—know better. We are less motivated by facts than by the mythological systems we are socialized into. So though improved information is certainly an important ingredient for shaping an Earth Democracy, a strategy based on data alone will not alter or change behavior. We need to look more closely at not what people think about, but how they think about and see the world.

As was argued previously, this is primarily the function of media operating within the ideology of the world system: corporate powers have the ability to shape how we think about the world by reinforcing a particular symbolic order and by promoting a particular subjectivity. Organic media practitioners will have to navigate this very powerful process through developing an awareness of how these conditions come to shape a personal media ecotone. Media are an environment, a commons like a national park. This commons has resources that colonizers seek. That resource is our attention. The portal to this commons is usually the screen—it both screens out and allows us to view in.

The world system occupies our senses through the consumer sublime, but it also symbolically occupies our cultural commons through its myth-making machinery. Given that the planetary mediasphere comprises a complex mix of grassroots media activism, DIY media, and corporate offerings, what happens when they overlap? James Cameron's 2009 global blockbuster film, *Avatar,* raises such a question. On the surface, *Avatar* is a typical monocultural product of the culture industry. Its production, marketing, product tie-ins, and normal hoo-ha that accompanies blockbuster films point to just another example of the world system appropriating mythological tropes. Moreover the film has been criticized as a New Age fantasy that demeans indigenous cultures. Yet undeniably audiences reacted profoundly to the movie, making it history's highest grossing film and spurning a variety of responses that make it an interesting case study.

The film's first scene begins with the protagonist's eyes opening to a world turned upside down, one in which the symbolic order is out of sorts and must be restored to balance. By the end of the film the world returns to its proper order, closing with the same protagonist's eyes staring back at us, but this time they have been transformed into those of some kind of hybrid creature. It is a road map for problem solving and spiritual transformation: from beginning to end we voyage through one of Hollywood's most tried and true narrative arcs, in which a reluctant hero goes through a series of tests before guiding the ruptured world back to its true essence. In this case, the film presents two paradigm extremes: the world system and anima mundi. The former is represented by the alien colonial forces attempting to conquer a planet, and the latter by its native inhabitants, the Na'vi. Bridging these cultures are characters with feet in both worlds: the colonial soldier, Sully, a wounded hero who becomes a shaman, and the Na'vi chief's daughter, Neytiri, who is schooled in the language of the oppressor. The love between them becomes a conduit for transformation.

Setting up the conflict in such black and white terms has its problems. As a kind of sci-fi version of a cowboy and Indians weekend matinee movie, Cameron plugged and played a number of tropes, the most obvious coming from films like *The Last of the Mohicans, Pocahontas,* and *Dances with Wolves.* In the end we have an updated version of the White Messiah violently intervening to resolve a conflict between pastoral natives and a colonial war machine. The bloody battle at the end of the film makes for good action sequences, but is it in keeping with a kind of transformative conflict resolution necessary for our age? Certainly the film's decisive battle scene would mesh with anti-civilization "primitivists" that call for bringing the fight to Empire. Though the film's final battle sequence does not represent the most creative approach to decolonization, self-defense is a legitimate response to colonial destruction. Ultimately the film's genre mash-up and conventions serve to create an easily digestible morality play that makes its ecological themes unambiguous.

Yet there is a danger of over-simplifying complexity, as well. Narrow representations have the potential effect of enclosing the imagination. For example, fantasy movies like *Harry Potter* inspire kids to consider the magical possibilities of the world, but what happens when during play children prefer to buy a merchandized magic wand than use a stick found in the park? *Avatar* could stimulate a sense of enchantment with nature, but will it be limited if children rely on the predigested images of the film and attendant merchandising to connect with the environment? Moreover, given the ecological theme of the movie one has to wonder (tongue jammed into cheek) if the disposable 3-D glasses given out at the theater are made of biodegradable plastic (they are imprinted with recycling symbol 7—which usually means unrecyclable). And then there are the plastic encased *Avatar* figurines distributed with McDonald's Happy Meals. Clearly the culture industry's machinery isn't going to just shut itself down in the wake of the world's greatest blockbuster. It may be too much to ask for Hollywood to purify itself of its own business model, but at least we (the audience) can make a critical intervention by supplying a deeper systems analysis when one is absent. This is what it means to take a media text and to turn it into an object-to-think-with.

Despite these inconsistencies, *Avatar* is a good example for how to resolve the contradictions between the world system and anima mundi. The quandary is that in order for the film to connect alienated viewers to nature spirits, it must use the technology of the system that it critiques. For example, Pandora's alien miners deploy 3-D imaging to map and exploit the world, while the film uses the same technology to exploit the apparent contradiction between technology and nature. Ecology to us modern folks is contradictory in the same way: we call for a return to nature, yet depend on science to map the risk of global peril in order to combat it. For instance, the iconic photo of Earth in space could not have been made possible without NASA, the same space agency that deploys a highly extractive and environmentally destructive form of "high" technology (U.S. rocket fuel is very destructive to the ozone and its toxic compounds are found in baby milk). At our current stage of globalization, arguments for restoring the biosphere, mitigation, and remediation, whether we like it or not, require science and technology, and even the internet, a primary by-product of military research. The rub is that technology, according to critic Jacques Ellul, is first a product of "technique," a way of rationalizing and categorizing the world that is materially manifested in technology. The bind is that we are now called upon to turn technique upon itself in order to tunnel back to "nature," something that is itself now just a cultural construct.

The internet is often used in popular culture as a synecdoche for planetary connectivity. *Avatar* takes that one step further by showing how Pandora is itself a kind of organic internet, its native inhabitants "jacking in" like the cyberpunk cowboys of William Gibson novels. So while it's true the system that produced the technology of *Avatar* is itself destructive, at the same time we should also acknowledge that it offers an emotional reconnection with planetary consciousness, its 3-D heart reaching out to us over the silhouetted heads of the theater.

The film depicts different manifestations of technological prosthetics. There are the machinery versions of the *RoboCop* variety deployed by the colonial military force, and there is the Avatar Project, which allows humans to control biologically engineered clones in order to infiltrate Pandora's natives. Finally there is the film itself, which is a prosthetic of our enlarged senses. Like us, the film's avatars are digital natives, which inhabit a hybrid domain of modern network technology and the primeval matrix of interconnectivity. Despite the popular belief that we are disconnected from the natural world (reflected by the fact that we talk as if there is a dichotomy between the two), like the film's avatars we are biologically and imminently part of the biosphere. We are not *on* Earth, we are *in* Earth. And just as my mirror neurons enable me to empathize and connect with fellow humans, they also extend to other animals, plants, and minerals. We are naturally interweaving with all aspects of our world, but due to our domestication (best symbolized by *Avatar*'s comically named antagonist, Parker Selfridge), we are trained to experience nature as if it were alien. The characters that navigate the avatars extend their awareness into a larger reality that hybridizes visualization technology (media!) with an empathic connection with the anima mundi represented by Pandora. As such, they are bridgers because they have feet in different worlds, thereby becoming conduits of empathy and translation between them.

But not everyone who deploys or encounters such bridging technologies will automatically feel the connection. The technological net that encompasses Pandora that models and maps it in 3-D fails to garner empathy for the colonial world eaters because of how it distances and virtualizes living systems. This serves the same function of dehumanization strategies used by the military that depend on euphemisms to depersonalize violence, such as the term "bug splat" for unintended civilian deaths. It's only through hybridization with the primal matrix that empathy becomes possible. In the case of *Avatar,* this occurs through technological bonding with the world's natives, who are themselves a kind of animal hybrid (though they wouldn't see themselves that way). Indeed, humans are animals too, lest we forget. Na'vi are part cat, part humanoid, which invokes some of Donna Haraway's work about cyborgs and hybridity. On a biological level, if we were pressed to evaluate what is it that defines us as human, we would be shocked to learn how much of us really is an emergent mix of trillions of minute transactions between more organisms that we can count. Moreover, our DNA contains even the most ancient strains of evolution. Indeed we are part lizard, bird, fish, and algae. Where the distinction begins and ends is cultural.

In order for us to reach beyond the reality bubble of technique, we start by burrowing our way through with what we can grasp. When Sully enters the world of the Na'vi for the first time, the only way he knows how to survive in the "alien" landscape is to use fire—our first technology. But it is only when the flame is extinguished that he can see the world alive with light and energy.

Avatar defamiliarizes the concept of "alien." As the dialogue and schematic shows, the humans are clearly the aliens, in the same sense that when the Spanish invaded the Americas, they too were aliens.

The film's machines—as cartoony as they are—are literal world eaters, visual manifestations of the very system that exists in our planet, right now, be they rain forest–consuming corporations or imperial invasions (references to mercenaries and "Shock and Awe" might confuse some of the film's fans who don't see Pandora's connection with Vietnam, Iraq, or Afghanistan). *Avatar*'s weakness is to not elaborate more on the RDA Corporation's home society. Like the war machine we see on the evening news, they are decontextualized from history. It would be more courageous if their parent "civilization" was identified as a democracy. That could help us see more directly how our own way of life is connected to the world-consuming ways of Pandora's colonizers.

Ultimately *Avatar*'s contribution to the mediasphere is how it helped reconnect the signifier chain between symbols and nature. The concept of a broken signifier chain, common to postmodern debates, relates to when symbols become disconnected from their source. The famous portrait of Che Guevara, for example, increasingly becomes disassociated from his original life as a revolutionary to become associated with style. Such "empty signifiers" become drained of meaning in order to be repurposed in any context. In a commodities or propaganda system, all representations have the potential to be disconnected from their original context. The ultimate example of a broken signifier chain is how economics are disassociated from ecology. From an economic perspective, for instance, the world is often represented by mathematical symbols, sign systems (like stock tickers), charts, and graphs. *Avatar* also depends on computing systems to generate its own visual representations, but rather than abstract living systems, it builds upon symbolic resources to reconstitute a transformative myth in order to reignite a global eco-spiritual perspective.

Blue Beings Occupy the Cultural Commons

Avatar inhabits a digital world so it can be copied, remixed, shared, and interacted with in ways that are unimaginable. Once *Avatar* became a global blockbuster, a number of previously ignored causes became visible in the mediasphere. *Avatar* catalyzed remixes, discussion boards, online communities, and solidarity movements, the kinds of participatory practices discussed by Henry Jenkins. People could take the movie and re-contextualize it with real-life examples. For example, when Palestinian activists donned Na'vi outfits during a protest, they translated their cause into a new symbolic order, recontextualizing their plight through the novel set of signs generated by *Avatar*. Thus, the reality frames of the past—which often portray Palestinians as extremists or terrorists—can be challenged by deploying the *Avatar* meme. Paradoxically, by associating themselves with the indigenous struggle of Pandora, Palestinian youth were also connecting themselves with global pop culture, a hybridized strategy that maneuvers aikido-like around the political controls normally exercised in the mainstream news media that rely on government frames to shape their struggle's narrative. By drawing upon the new planetary myth generated by *Avatar*, Palestinians made their plight—ironically—more real to Europeans and Americans. This is important because outsiders' uncritical support of Israel contributes to the suffering of Palestinians.

Likewise, an indigenous group in India, the Dongria Kondh, used *Avatar*'s symbolism to fight Vedanta Resources's mining operation that threatened their holy mountain. The Dongria Kondh's situation more closely parallels *Avatar*, which did not escape the attention of Survival International, an NGO that helps protect other endangered tribal groups. In an appeal they sent to James Cameron for support, Survival International directly framed the tribal struggle against a British mining concern in the following terms:

> Avatar is fantasy . . . and real.
> The Dongria Kondh tribe in India are struggling to defend their land against a mining company hell-bent on destroying their sacred mountain.

Please help the Dongria.
We've watched your film—now watch ours.

To make the point more clear, in 2010 demonstrators in blue makeup and Na'vi prosthetics protested in London outside the mining concern's headquarters. As a result of the public pressure put on shareholders and the Indian government, in 2010 the Dongria Kondh won their battle against Vedanta. The proposed mining project was scrapped. Was it because of *Avatar*? This is impossible to prove, but unquestionably *Avatar* gave the Dongria Kondh symbolic resources that didn't exist before the film reached a global audience.

Although these protests might strike some as just image events designed for the planetary spectacle—after all, much of the work of environmental activist groups like Greenpeace is staging image events—the worldwide mediasphere is still the main theater of global action. Though media generally claim to represent the world, mediators are usually only accountable to the extent that they remain "credible" according to the conventions of professional ethics. Because media are a source of reality construction, the *Avatar* meme became a symbolic resource that could be redistributed to redress the misrepresentation or absence of other actors who also make up the world's population.

Even though such symbolic actions are directed toward getting the attention of media managers, policy makers, or other mediators who have the power to do something about the problem of media representation, colonized people have long recognized that survival often means mastering the language of the oppressors, including the visual. In the past the strategy would be to become literate in the colonizer's written and spoken language, but now the necessity is to repurpose global communication strategies. Consequently, often rights battles also become semiotic struggles, as was the case of the Mi'kmaq fight for land rights in Nova Scotia. In court battles to protect their lands, Native American activists donned traditional clothes to legitimize to outsiders that their perspective represented the "sacred." Unfortunately, in our culture, in the public arena someone dressed like a lawyer cannot claim a religious right to the land, but someone who "looks Indian" can. Likewise, the simple tropes and genre mash-ups of *Avatar* played a similar role to make the film's morality play even more obvious and digestible within established pop culture rules that provide little space for alternative representations of the sacred.

In order for indigenous people to place their struggle within a global context (and hence get attention for their cause from the external people who can assist) they have to contend with preexisting symbolic resources in the semiosphere that are markers for planetary citizenship and ecology. Aside from the "noble savage" stereotypes of literature and film (which also fill *Avatar*'s screen), there are few examples of media that fuse technology, indigenous struggle, global survival, and the sacred. But now the image of Na'vi fits into an approach already developed by global activists, which is to draw on planetary symbols for collective action and empathy. To this end, we can expect to see more blue people appearing on Earth in the very near future.

Though *Avatar*'s ultimate impact on global ecological consciousness remains to be seen, it offers a hopeful alternative to the uglier visions of the future offered by fearmongering corporate media. New myths and stories that promote planetary consciousness will be necessary to remediate our varied ecotones that have been unduly shaped by the monocultural paradigm.

Admittedly, the social and economic structure makes alternative practices difficult and therefore appears inevitable and unstoppable. It takes the mentality of a spiritual warrior to engage in radical practice, such as eschewing cars, airplanes, plastics, or toxic electronics. To operate on that level of mindfulness is difficult work and only few are up to the task. Most people will have to find a way within their means to negotiate the complexities of the world system without being overly complicit in its self-destructive path. On the most primary level, our most powerful tool is attention. Inattention to the exploitative nature of the world system's invasive technique is how it perpetuates itself. Like the gardener we will need to attend carefully to the various conditions of our environment, being mindful of those characteristics that reproduce the world system consciousness within ourselves and also aware of those positive and useful qualities that are part of our ancient heritage and that remain alive and strong.

CHAPTER 6

Mediating an Earth Democracy

One of the starker images to emerge from the London riots of Summer 2011 was a hooded youth donning 100 percent Adidas attire in the midst of burning cars. It startled me because just a few years ago Adidas had launched a viral ad campaign that specifically identified its brand with a particular kind of urban rebellion: guerilla gardening. Technically guerrilla gardening is "gardening someone else's land without permission." It could be a vacant lot, a meridian, or neglected property. As a kind of direct action it is political in nature, for it relocalizes control and also facilitates local food production. Guerrilla gardening should be an activity associated with decolonizing media because like its cousin, graffiti art, it's a way of reappropriating public space and hence the commons.

Adidas created a short viral video that was posted on YouTube featuring its own version of guerilla gardening. It depicts youths scaling fences while using GPS, night vision, and an assortment of other TV crime show devices. The video is accompanied by quasi-seventies-era bongo suspense music to give it a tongue-and-cheek feel. As the narrative develops, the youths find an appropriate place to start their garden, then they go to a big box store to purchase their materials. After planting a very picturesque and orderly garden, they go on their way, presumably to leave it to the elements without a plan for maintenance.

As to be expected, Adidas neuters the phenomenon of any politics and disregards all the elements that go into a successful gardening. Gardens are cultivated within specific ecological niches that require the shared knowledge and practices of a community's collective intelligence. Gardens are not simply purchased from the box store and then transplanted into the urban landscape like an advertisement. Adidas probably thinks that guerrilla gardening is disconnected from a serious critique of business as usual. Which brings me back to the photo. Adidas, and other apparel companies like it, have no ethical dilemma pirating street cred to sell their products. But what happens when apolitical faux rebellion is translated into the real urban landscape where youth have no real access to the aspirations that are marketed to them? Adidas wants the aura of authentic rebellion, but can the company and the globalized commodities system it depends on withstand rebellion when it actually transpires?

By contrast, an appropriate response to colonial power is the media equivalent of biomimicry, which seeks to emulate relationships in natural systems. Concurrently, sustainable design solutions should not be about creating less unsustainable behavior but coming up with solutions that solve many problems at once, including how we think about the world. For instance, less unsustainability in the form of fuel-efficient cars does not mean we are creating a post-oil society based on ecological values.

To give a media example, an organization called Eco Media partnered with the TV network CBS to brand certain ads it airs with a green leaf logo that indicates the advertiser is contributing part of its ad fee to some kind of sustainable community project. So when the car manufacturer Chevrolet donated money to build a "green" playground in Arlington, Texas, its TV ads were branded with the Eco Media logo. Such an approach represents "shallow" ecology, a kind of anthropocentric approach to sustainability that fails to break from the paradigm at the source of unsustainable cultural behaviors because it doesn't fundamentally challenge the paradigm of economic growth and consumption promoted by marketing. Rather, Eco Media helps the commodities system greenwash itself without providing a legitimate, sustainable alternative. As long as we have media driven by car advertising, the fundamental energy paradigm of the media ecosystem will remain trapped in the carbon economy.

By contrast, examples abound reflecting a deeper effort to green media, many of which are more deserving of an "eco media" label than a Chevrolet ad. For example, Annie Leonard's partnership with the social marketing and animation outfit Free Range Studio resulted in the wildly popular Story of Stuff Project. What first started out as a twenty-minute video posted on their website and YouTube has now spawned half a dozen animated shorts that deconstruct from an ecosystems perspective various aspects of our commodities system. Its website is a veritable hub of activism, featuring maps for community screenings, an events calendar, curricula, annotated scripts with resources and research, and a linking mechanism for the social web so that teachers or activists can incorporate these educational videos into their work. Translated into over fifteen languages and seen by more than twelve million people, in essence these animations are like seed packages that can be planted in a variety of contexts to promote sustainability. As a sign of the Project's success, various Fox News programs and right wing media producers have sought to discredit its environmental perspective though spurious flak claiming the Project promotes an anti-growth message. Indeed!

The Climate Reality Project offers another alternative to Eco Media's approach. As a successor to Al Gore's *An Inconvenient Truth,* in 2011 the Project produced a twenty-five-minute slide show that was shown on the internet over a twenty-four-hour period during an event they dubbed 24 Hours of Reality. Each hour featured a presentation from a specific time zone. The presentations were localized, but also maintained a global perspective by connecting the various unusual weather events around the world to a common pattern that clearly showed the link between increased flooding and massive storm systems and the changing chemistry of our atmosphere. But more brilliantly, engaging in a kind of media literacy exercise, the presentation picked apart each red herring thrown out by the climate deniers, taking a page from the anti-tobacco movement to show that a systematic disinformation campaign has been launched by the fossil fuel industry to discredit climate science. The Project's website features sharable videos from each event, including two short informational documentaries that link the efforts of the tobacco industry to suppress health research with current anti-climate change campaigns. It, too, is in over a dozen languages and offers the chance to request a speaker to give the presentation at a local event.

Likewise, the environmental activist and writer Bill McKibben advocates for the media equivalent of a farmers' market. Citing a study that shows that farmers' markets are more likely to generate conversations between strangers than supermarkets, he suggests that media can serve a similar purpose, not only by bringing disparate people together, but by also having a strong local component that ties together regional issues with planetary causes. Key to his analysis is the distinction he makes between "box store" economics driven by quantity and efficiency versus local economies based on quality and decentralization. In terms of a media strategy, McKibben practices what he preaches by helping establish 350.org, a web hub designed to promote a global grassroots movement focused on a singular goal: returning our current atmospheric emissions to 350 parts per million CO_2, which is the agreed limit for humanity to live safely (as of this writing we are at 392). The website combines organizing tools with informational animations, user-generated media, activist tools, scientific facts, and calls for action. In 2011 the organization was on the frontlines of organized civil disobedience against the Keystone pipeline project and is likely the reason why the U.S. government ended up backing off its support. 350.org makes and distributes media, but it also facilitates live encounters during coordinated days of action when people gather in their communities to bring attention to the cause. Often these events draw on local creativity and art. For example, in Santa Fe, New Mexico, a group created a human "flash flood" (a kind of artistic flash mob) in a dry riverbed where water should be flowing. In a video posted on YouTube one can see the multicultural character of the event, which included Native American dancers, Hispano musicians, puppets, performers, kids, and many diverse folks from the community.

Additionally, listener-supported community radio often has a kind of farmers' market vibe. KUNM in Albuquerque, New Mexico, for example, combines feeds from global news agencies and citizen journalists with local coverage that serves Native Americans, Hispanics, and various other listeners. One of its regular feeds is the nationally syndicated program, Democracy Now! With over a thousand stations in its network, Democracy Now! hybridizes its radio broadcast as a parallel television feed that can be seen on Link TV and Free Speech TV. It also archives and distributes its programming on the web. Because they are audience-sponsored, they are not dependent on corporate or government funding the way that more mainstream public news networks such as PBS, NPR, and BBC are.

In contrast to Facebook and Google+, alternative online social networks are self-consciously committed to raising consciousness or promoting activism. Based on the open source software platform Drupal, Evolver.net (created by the same folks who publish its sister site, Reality Sandwich) hosts a user-generated portal that is subscription-driven. In order to promote "conscious collaboration," the network's members share resources (tools, services), start initiatives, promote causes, disseminate news, and organize regional "spores" for meet-and-greet events and "cultural incubation." Likewise, author and environmental activist Paul Hawken initiated WiserEarth.org, an online social network designed to connect people and groups working for environmental and social justice (WISER stands for World Index of Social and Environmental Responsibility). Based on his work in *Blessed Unrest,* Hawken argues that globally over a million disparate organizations are working simultaneously (but not necessarily consciously connected) to solve environmental and social justice problems, the biggest movement in the history of humanity. His site, like the many described here, enable these different groups to network, exchange ideas, and link together in the best possible sense of cross-cultural pollination that will enable us to solve our planetary crisis.

Finally, the act of making media should in and of itself be sustainable. Several groups have formed to address the waste generated by media industries. Indy record labels like Earthology, Green Owl, and Smog Veil have dedicated themselves to greening their entire production process. Steps include using salvaged materials for building recording studios, incorporating Earth-friendly materials into their merchandise, and using renewable energy. Some bands have committed to reducing their carbon footprint while touring, either by using biodiesel powered vehicles or purchasing carbon offsets. Music gatherings like the Bonnaroo Music and Arts Festival have committed to waste reduction, green power, and supporting sustainable vendors and activist groups. A project initiated by the green music nonprofit Reverb, Green Music Group (www.greenmusicgroup.org) is a coalition supporting efforts to green the music industry by offering a variety of resources, including ideas for greening transportation, catering, waste reduction, lodging, and merchandise. Likewise, people are organizing to green the film and TV industry, a massively wasteful and toxic production process (also see the Environmental Media Association, www.ema-online.org). New Zealand's Greening the Screen (www.greenthescreen.co.nz) offers good pointers for environmentally responsible practices. Various film boards around the world also push for standards and best practices. Several major media companies have additionally taken on green initiatives (such as Disney, NBCUniversal, and News Inc.), but industry efforts to police themselves remain suspect, serving more to greenwash their operations than fundamentally altering their business model.

The difference between Eco Media and these examples of alternative media is that the former attempts to reinforce the status quo—a closed media ecosystem that serves the interests of the carbon economy—and the latter are networked into an open media ecosystem designed to create greater connectivity (as opposed to greater disconnectivity). In essence, these alternative media practices are akin to a kind of media permaculture. When applied to gardening, permaculture varies according to its different practitioners, but there are a number of commonly agreed upon approaches that can be followed in order to execute appropriately scaled design. Such steps serve as good prompts for thinking about media permaculture, and mirror the kind of design that went into the various examples described here. According to Patrick Whitefield, when initiating a permaculture project people need to map current conditions, survey the site, find out what the inhabitants want to do with the site (and what skills they can offer), evaluate the research, draw up a proposal (including a map), and then make a final re-evaluation. All of these stages resemble the kinds of actions taken by the Occupy movement. In the case of Occupy Wall Street in lower Manhattan, permaculture was incorporated into the campsite, including the use of human-powered generators to power electronics. The particular conditions of the site called for appropriate media strategies, including the deployment of cardboard signs, banners, online streaming, and documentation with cell phones and online collaborative tools. Every step involved people consulting each other and mapping the site tactically and philosophically.

From Slow Food to Slow Media

It's important to promote slower, ritual forms of media that can bring people together in real time and in physical space. To envision how this could work, we can draw from the slow food movement. Slow food emerged in Italy as a response to the invasion of fast food culture. Its slogan, "eat your view," means people should eat food that exists within their particular landscape horizon. It attempts to preserve the cultural commons associated with food by eschewing monocultural agricultural methods (including genetically modified seeds). It promotes cooking and eating together, organic farming techniques, preserving heirloom seeds, growing locally, and treating livestock humanely.

As I've been arguing, with media our view—what we look at and engage—is continually being eaten by the media portals that give us access. Media, however, have an unlimited horizon, so our attention often gets sucked into a kind of void that is easily commoditized. By redrawing attention to local concerns and reality, and grounding media to service these conditions, our attention no longer becomes food for corporations.

For example, by combining a critical documentary with discussion and food, we can move from a transmission model of media to one based on ritual. Imagine a food film festival featuring a documentary like *Food, Inc.* Shot as an independent feature-length film, *Food, Inc.* set out to debunk the myths about the U.S. food system using a holistic approach to the problem. Drawing heavily on the journalist Michael Pollan's book *The Omnivore's Dilemma, Food, Inc.* opens with Pollan deconstructing food packaging and supermarket design. The film then breaks down the differences between the centralized, industrialized food system and sustainable agricultural practices. Making connections between the role of government regulation, immigrant labor, animal abuse, corporate monopolization, food prices, and nutrition, its systems-wide metaview was so startling that the filmmaker spent much of his budget on legal fees to protect himself from frivolous lawsuits.

Though a conventional documentary in the sense that it was meant to be screened in theaters and festivals, *Food, Inc.* got legs through a variety of partnerships, including promotions by Stonyfield Farm (which is featured in the film) and Chipotle. But more importantly, through special screenings the film could be used to generate discussion and to connect global issues with local food production. In a public meeting space or at farmers' markets people could screen the film while also creating a space for growers to connect with people. Likewise, any documentary of interest can be screened at house parties. Such is the strategy of Brave New Films, which encourages people to sign up on its website to host screening events at homes, bookstores, cafés, libraries, classrooms, and other community venues. These grassroots distribution efforts bypass the traditional studio system, connecting people with people and ideas.

This ties into the thinking of the social critic Ivan Illich, who called for us to develop "tools for conviviality." By conviviality, Illich means tools that serve "politically interrelated individuals" as opposed to "managers." Such tools, in his view, have responsible boundaries placed on them. In other words, they honor natural limits. Illich applied his thinking to a number of institutions, such as health care and education. Before such terms were used in our current debate about the internet, he advocated open networks ("learning webs") over closed systems ("manipulative institutions"). In his particular vision, community centers would be networking hubs for people to find skilled practitioners who could teach them particular skills, such as how to play guitar, cook, or fix things. Interestingly, many websites do serve such a function, representing the more egalitarian and practical side of the internet that encourages informal learning and networking that circumvent traditional media and educational institutions.

Illich would likely concur with media theorist David Gauntlett's idea that "making is connecting." Gauntlett observes that the early Web resembled a series of walled gardens, but through the advent of social media (Web 2.0), the facilitation of easy interconnectivity has turned the web into a kind of "communal allotment" where all these gardens connect. People all over the world make stuff and can share their skills, interests, and knowledge through the communal nature of the interconnected web. The one-size-fits-all version of monoculture is seriously disrupted when people's voices can be heard and when we can connect with and share disparate voices. While it's true that such voices on the internet are not as diverse as the planetary community, organizations like Rising Voices promote new tools and communities around translation and language preservation that help diversify communications platforms. Rather than a global village, maybe what we need is a planetary food festival and jam session. The main point is that if we use food as a guiding metaphor, we can evolve media strategies that mimic the ultimate intersection between humans and living systems.

Toward an Ethical Spectacle

The repurposing of *Avatar* motifs by global activists demonstrates the evolving role of how "image events" determine the news. Scholar Kevin DeLuca argues that the model of hegemonic media predicts that news coverage of environmental activists will portray them as "deviants" that violate market fundamentalism and social norms. In most cases news coverage actually does this. But DeLuca believes it doesn't matter because our current postmodern environment has destabilized a number of cultural myths, which has created a new space for environmental ideas to subvert hegemonic news production. To back this claim he points out that the agenda of so-called radical environmentalism remains popular when polled among the general public (however, in recent years we see a steady reversal as a result of the carbon industry's disinformation campaign to discredit climate change). The advantage postmodern ecoactivists have over industrial media practice comes down to the difference between strategy and tactics. In reference to French sociologist Michel de Certeau's *The Practice of Everyday Life,* DeLuca argues that "strategy" means engaging centers of power (i.e., Washington, DC) and arguing within the frame of hegemonic (industrial) definitions of nature, such as "protecting" it as a "resource" separate from humans. But at the core of postmodernism is the destabilization of nature as a concept. Many global activists who took up the *Avatar* meme in their own struggles are "disorganizations" which fall outside the normal discursive structures of media frames that prefer to deal with formal organizations (like Sierra Club) or government sources. Decentralized activist groups then can be "tactical." They are not subject to the rules of "strategy," so they can flexibly form their identities, name the world, and challenge constructions of reality.

Likewise, one way global activists can draw on planetary memes to effect change is through what activist Stephen Duncombe calls the "ethical spectacle." He argues for new media practices that move beyond the confines of conventional media and journalism by turning to alternative responses that work outside the normal frames of media. He starts with the premise that political spectacles (fascist and communist alike) are similar to advertising in that they all make mythical claims while being undemocratic by design. Citing the quintessential example of Leni Riefenstahl's Nazi propaganda film, *Triumph of the Will,* we see that spectators are allowed to participate (as in the choreographed movements of the SS), but they are not involved in the construction or design of the spectacle. Spectacle is not open, and it lacks spontaneity and surprise (even Janet Jackson's 2004 Super Bowl wardrobe "malfunction" and M.I.A.'s 2012 middle finger flap have to be suspected as publicity pranks).

In the "ethical spectacle" participants become "co-producer" and "co-director" of the spectacle. In this regard Duncombe argues that "nonintervention" and "transformative action" are better terms—or what game designers call "transformative play." One tactic is satire, because jokes and humor are participatory activities—you have to get the joke to understand it, which means you are participating in its meaning through shared cultural practices. Jokes are social. In this sense the Palestinian activists were engaged in a deadly serious joke, with their use of Na'vi attire having a humorous edge. The 2011 meme that remixed the image of Lt. John Pike pepper spraying UC Davis protestors became an instantaneous internet joke used to critique oppressive policing. Given that the Na'vi trope now has extended reach, the event that the Palestinians staged had a participatory quality, as evidenced by the number of blogs and media that responded to it.

Duncombe calls for "open spectacle," which builds on Umberto Eco's concept of the *opera aperta*—a work that is open to interpretation and completed by the viewer. Like the open nature of the Occupy movement, it's messy and doesn't have confined meaning, but emerges through participation. Moreover, open spectacle is also transparent in nature. By contrast, fascist spectacle and ads refer to themselves as reality, but the reality they represent is self-referential and does not achieve the utopian images they aspire to. Ethical spectacle seeks to be transparent through being self-reflexive, such as the technique of German playwright Bertolt Brecht's V-effect, or "alienation effect" (more "aha" and less "oooh"), which seeks to draw attention to the production process. An example of this is seen in how the various Occupy movements used participatory media practices (see below). Another is a flash mob, such as when groups use social media to coordinate interventions for the purpose of entertainment, performance art, or protesting. Flash mobs can be pillow fights in the middle of a busy train station, or protestors eating ice cream silently in public squares in protest against laws that prohibit public gatherings. Howard Rheingold's variation of this is "smart mobs," which use social media to enhance collective intelligence. Regardless of the particular strategy, when activists echo and remix *Avatar*'s tropes or the image of Lt. Pike pepper-spraying protestors, an ethical spectacle emerges, transitioning the symbolic order from the closed system of the Hollywood culture industry or traditional news framing conventions to the open system of globalized participatory culture.

Three Scenarios for Media Ecosystems

The market credo of neoliberalism favors deregulation and monopolization, which ultimately leads to increased centralization and dependence on media cartels for our communication needs. The democratization of access and usage of the net requires vigilance, activism, organizing, policy, and practice that discourages the lockdown of communications tools and promotes open systems.

The political theorist Benjamin Barber argues that

when it comes to media systems we face three potential futures: Pangloss (complacency), Pandora (worst-case), and Jeffersonian (nurturing democracy). Pangloss represents the status quo in which the current systems in place maintain their momentum. It's a mixed bag that includes both nefarious corporate practices and emerging egalitarian uses of media. The status quo represents a do-nothing attitude, which favors prevailing factors. As such it would likely enable market-based approaches and policies to such issues as the digital divide and intellectual property. It means less regulation, more privatization, and greater monopolization of the cultural commons. But if you like using Facebook, Twitter, and Google, they are part of this scenario as well.

If these conditions are allowed to prevail without active citizen engagement, we will most likely enter the Pandora scenario, which represents the worst-case outcome of current trends. The way that WikiLeaks was essentially censored by private companies is an example of what this scenario looks like. Recall that after WikiLeaks released a series of U.S. government classified documents that revealed private communications between State Department officials in 2010/2011, various internet services created a virtual blockade against WikiLeaks. First, denial of service attacks were waged against the organization's domain address. This strategy, initially developed by hackers, overwhelms Web host servers with page requests, making the website essentially inaccessible. Next, EveryDNS, which is responsible for associating domain names with

IP addresses, blocked WikiLeaks.org from being accessed on the web. Then Amazon.com booted WikiLeaks from its servers. Meanwhile, MasterCard, Visa, and PayPal stopped processing donations. Apple also disabled the WikiLeaks iPhone app that enabled people to read its content. Finally, government agencies blocked employees from accessing or discussing WikiLeaks materials. All of these combined effectively censored WikiLeaks, privatizing that which the government couldn't do through the court system. These actions are not that different from how information on the web is controlled in China, the difference being that it was private businesses that engaged in self-censorship as opposed to following direct orders from the government. Other aspects of the Pandora scenario include:

- *Greater intellectual property control through anti-piracy legislation which turns internet providers into copyright police.* For years governments have been negotiating the Anti-Counterfeiting Trade Agreement *in secret.* This undemocratically written legislation would require internet providers to police their users, thereby privatizing civil law. The agreement also would empower drug companies to enforce patents to prevent generic, life-saving drugs from the marketplace. (This is a clear example of enclosure: drug development, which often takes place at publicly funded universities, gets patented by private companies.) Finally, such legislation is also tied to genetically modified organisms (GMOs), enforcing and restricting how seeds are used. This shows how media policy is not isolated from other economic trends, but is in fact interconnected with the broader colonial system. Similar bills sponsored by the entertainment industry are continually floated in the U.S. Congress and Senate. Vigilant and robust citizen activism (such as the internet strike of 2012 in which several websites like Wikipedia went dark in protest) have kept these bills in check. But as long as corporate IP holders get their wish to police the internet and the political system remains corrupted by corporate lobbying and cash, these proposals will continue to surface.

- *Digital rights management (DRM) that restricts and limits how people move files around between gadgets and the web.* A good example relates to how Amazon.com retains control and ownership of books for its e-reader, Kindle. In the past Amazon.com has remotely deleted books from Kindle users. Unlike books bought in a store, e-books cannot be traded, resold, or given away. Media files purchased through other services, such as iTunes, require proprietary software.

- *Increased government control, surveillance, and censorship à la the Great Fire Wall of China.* Throughout the world activist activities on the web have been censored officially or through pressure against private companies. Additionally, governments can monitor activist activities overtly (just by simple searches and reading Facebook), or covertly when they demand user data be turned over. Search engines could also be forced to filter out key words or sites that are deemed "rogue" or illegal.

■ *An increasingly limited public domain through the enclosure and privatization of the cultural commons.* Disney, for example, takes fairy tales from the public domain, creates its own versions and then copyrights them. Despite corporate media's presence in our daily lives, oftentimes even when their products become part of the commons, people are prohibited from freely incorporating these images or sounds into their daily practice. Proposed legislation includes jail sentences for anyone who streams copyrighted music on the internet. So if you wanted to record yourself lip-syncing your favorite song or create your own music videos for copyrighted music, you would be criminally liable.

■ *The elimination of alternative perspectives from media.* As discussed earlier, this is a normal process of hegemony. The *New York Times,* which republished and reported on WikiLeaks material, carefully distanced itself by marginalizing its founder and differentiating its activities from the rebel organization. This sets a dangerous precedent, because in essence, though WikiLeaks constitutes a legitimate form of journalism, the *New York Times* sought to de-legitimate WikiLeaks by associating it with criminal behavior.

■ *The reduction and elimination of open systems architecture.* Architecture is law, as net activists argue. All the activities described above represent closed, and hence colonial, behaviors. Closed systems, such as software and computers made by Apple, have the benefit of being bug-free, crash-proof, virus immune, and well designed. Yet the trade-off is that we have to depend on Apple's goodwill to protect the interests of consumers, workers, and the environment. Despite its elegant and efficient design, it has failed badly in most of these categories. The elimination of the WikiLeaks app is one such example; the blocking of other apps it deems amoral gives the company tremendous censorship powers. This represents a good metaphor for the national security state: many are willing to give up civil liberties for the sake of a safer, albeit more restricted, society. Big Media offer slick entertainment, interfaces, and programming, but their closed nature leaves little space for dissenting opinions.

Essentially, if the Pandora scenario comes to pass, civil law and the cultural commons will be enclosed and privatized.

The Jeffersonian scenario represents the democratic potential of media, but it is only feasible when we engage in active cultural citizenship. For example, the way some defenders and civil libertarians responded to the treatment of WikiLeaks represents aspects of how the hopeful model of the Jeffersonian scenario works. After it was cut off, WikiLeaks's web presence was maintained by a number of mirror sites that people voluntarily and fearlessly set up on the web. The hacker group Anonymous also used denial of service attacks against the corporations that blocked WikiLeaks. Meanwhile, media activists openly shamed and agitated against the offending organizations. WikiLeaks, whose philosophy is to impose transparency upon opaque power structures, was able to sustain a presence throughout the mediasphere as bloggers, Twitterers, and sharers reverberated and amplified revelations from the leaks. Unfortunately, these activities combined did little to prevent Wikileak's demise. Ultimately, when the cultural commons is privatized, the public has little control or recourse to reverse the decisions of corporations who ultimately control how money and data is distributed on the web.

Ideally the Jeffersonian scenario is buttressed by the participatory cultural practices of the social Web. Such activities and principles include:

- *Culture jamming.* Culture jamming, which has been around since Dada, is an activist strategy that seeks to disrupt the symbolic order through sabotaging and reconstituting previously existing media. Culture jamming has been mainstreamed through mash-ups and remixing, an aesthetic practice so common now that even marketers are using it. Nonetheless, it remains a potent tool of appropriation. Popular culture from *Avatar* to *V for Vendetta* to *Sesame Street* can be recontextualized to create new meanings and broader cultural awareness.

- *Hactivism.* Hactivism comes in many forms, including culture jamming (which is largely symbolic, like billboard defacement), pranking (designed to reveal media hypocrisy), illegal disruptions of existing computer systems (such as the activities of Anonymous), graffiti (hacking public space), "identity correction" (a kind of hoaxing perpetrated by the Yes Men in which activists impersonate corporate representatives), comedy, and flash mobs (another form of hacking public space). According to Steven Levi, hackers embody an ethic that includes sharing, openness, decentralization, free access to computers, and world improvement. Ultimately, when done on behalf of the public good, hactivism is a kind of electronic civil disobedience.

- *Cultural engagement based on* read-write, *as opposed to* read-only, *activities*. This characterizes intellectual property scholar Lawrence Lessig's model for how digital media has changed the nature of media economics. Read-only media are based on scarcity, with control maintained through the monopolization of production and copyright. With the internet serving as a digital copy machine, users can reproduce, share, splice, and remix anything that results from cultural production. Such practices already existed among artists and activists ranging from Dada to hip hop, but the normalization of remixing and mash-ups means that culture jamming has gone mainstream. Lessig argues for lenient and fair intellectual property rules that legalize common cultural practices. The danger, he argues, means criminalizing the everyday activities of Netizens.

- *Peer-to-peer (P2P) sharing*. This means that users can connect directly with each other through distributed networks without middlemen. Though attacked as a means for piracy (copyrighted music and films are shared through P2P technologies like BitTorrent), P2P is also an appropriate mode and metaphor for empowered democratic participation. P2P University, for example, allows anyone to propose and teach a course to the general public. "Commons-based peer production," coined by net theorist Yochai Benkler, represents networked distributed cultural production, as is the case of free and open source software Wikipedia or any other Wiki platforms. Finally, P2P allows artists to connect directly with their fans. Filmmakers, writers, and musicians use P2P to distribute their works without having to go through traditional media companies. In terms of activism, at the time of this writing Global Square, a hub that relies on Tribler's P2P technology to create an unbreakable activist network, is in development.

- *Self-organization.* Distributed and open networks create conditions for self-organization. As Clay Shirky argues, the internet enables easy group forming. This doesn't mean that it happens automatically. A bit of old-fashioned networking via personal communications helps build online communities, but rather than having to *push* media to get your message out, people *pull* media according to their interests. According to Shirky, three conditions are necessary for success: 1) a plausible promise (a good reason "why" we should join a network); 2) an effective tool ("how" it can be used matches our needs); and 3) an acceptable bargain between the users and host (if we accept the promise and use the tools, do our expectations correspond with those of the network creator?). Wikipedia represents a good example of this: the Wiki tool enables anyone to edit a page, and because so many people can access and edit it, the site gets built collectively by volunteers from across the globe. Another useful insight from Shirky is based on Chris Anderson's "long tail theory," which is that all user-generated sites have a small hardcore group of users that drive the network's content creation and use, but cumulative small inputs from periodic users add up to a greater whole. The reason open source and user generated media succeed is because the cost of failure is minimal; it's like the diversity of an ecosystem when there's a budget of flexibility that allows for evolutionary experiments to succeed.

- *Curation as an alternative to traditional journalism.* "Live blogs," for example, are used by traditional media companies to cull up-to-the-minute news from across the mediasphere, providing a live, real-time view of how events are played out and interpreted throughout the web. Likewise, news organizations, such as Al-Jazeera, hybridize their news gathering, drawing on user-generated media as source material for its reportage. As such, Al-Jazeera echoes throughout the mediasphere, amplifying voices that traditionally have been eschewed by the colonial media, such as those of Arab youths. Free news curation tools that bypass traditional news media include Storify (www.storify.com) and Scoop.it (www.scoop.it).

- *Mind amplification.* This denotes Howard Rheingold's concept for how net tools extend and amplify intelligence. Personal learning networks (PLN), for example, can be created through net "dashboards," portals like Netvibes that allow users to feed materials according to topics, key words, or people of interest (including yourself!). By building a PLN, one can self-educate through selectively following the brightest and most interesting mediators and curators on the web. Rheingold's caveat is that such an approach requires "crap detection," a kind of "infotention" that involves "tuning" and refining. An expert "mind amplifier" needs technical know-how (literacy of attention, participation, collaboration, and network savvy), knowing how to ask the right questions, and, of course, curiosity.

- *Creative Commons.* This represents an alternative to traditional copyright. Depending on the kind of license (there are three variations), those using the Creative Commons (www.creativecommons.org) scheme allow their works to be freely shared or remixed, thereby circumventing traditional intellectual control mechanisms. This is not to say copyright or trademarking should be abolished altogether—it can be an important protection against colonial powers. Indigenous groups argue, for example, that they may have little alternative than to invoke these rights when faced with corporations trying to patent their traditional herbal remedies. Nonetheless, as Lessig and other activists point out, the current intellectual property law favors corporations over the public interest. Initially copyright in the United States lasted for fourteen years, the idea being that it was enough time for the creator to benefit economically from his or her original works, but then that exclusive right would lapse to the public. The theory is that culture evolves and society benefits when it has full access to its brain trust. Current copyright law is the life of the author plus seventy-five years. As noted, such restrictive rules simply don't match the cultural practices of internet users.

- *Net neutrality.* Net neutrality guarantees that all data transfers on the web are treated equally, ensuring that no restrictions are made by internet providers. For example, proposals by media giants like Comcast (now majority shareholder of NBC) would create a two-tiered internet in which companies could decide which sites get faster access. In fact, it has been documented that some providers have slowed P2P sharing on their networks. Working to achieve diversity and equal access then becomes the task of media justice activists (see below).

- *Media Justice.* Those working for greater access to traditionally underserved communities often fall under the rubric of media justice. The primary concern is to reduce the *digital divide,* the division between the haves and have-nots of the digital commons. As much as we like to tout the benefits of the internet, it remains largely a tool for those who have access to broadband, technology, electricity, education, and technical know-how. Even as recently as the Arab Spring, spreading news on TV (such as Al-Jazeera) was as important as online social networks, because in most of the world, TV has far greater penetration—it's far easier to access and needs little technical expertise. Given the importance of the internet for circumventing colonial media, promoting access should be a priority for activists. Just as libraries are considered a public asset, municipal governments should support free wireless access. Not surprising, a key issue for media justice activists is stopping mergers and monopolization by telecommunications companies that threaten to dominate wireless access. In terms of the digital divide, there is also a "production gap," which represents those who have the skills to make media versus those who just consume it. Media justice advocates for community empowerment and decentralized media versus corporate control. An overarching theme of this activism is that communication is a human right. The Center for Media Justice (http://centerformediajustice.org), Media and Democracy Coalition (www.media-democracy.net), and Media Action Grassroots Network (http://mag-net.org) advocate diligently on this issue.

■ *Prosumers.* Prosumers blur the line between production and consumption. The availability of cheap high-definition video cameras and laptop editing software enables amateurs to produce professional quality media. Cellphone users can also make media on the fly. Such instantaneous forms of citizen journalism have been instrumental for documenting the activities of the Arab Spring and Occupy movements. This trend represents the flip side of surveillance: the watchers are empowered to watch the watchmen. In this sense, citizen journalism represents a significant development in the balance of power between corporate and civic media. Dan Gillmor's *Medi-*

active book and website (www.mediactive.com) is a good starting place.

■ *Media literacy.* It's a given that our educational system promotes reading and writing as crucial skills for basic civic engagement. When it comes to media, however, few programs in the United States offer media literacy as a primary requirement. Approaches to media literacy vary, but at a minimum everyone should learn to critically engage media, use it creatively to tell stories, and know how to participate actively. The contents of this manifesto represent my particular approach to media literacy, but resources on the net abound. A few places to begin include the Media Literacy Project (www.medialiteracyproject.org), Center for Media Literacy (www.medialit.org), Action Coalition for Media Education (www.acmecoalition.org), National Association for Media Literacy Education (http://namle.net), Media Awareness Network (www.media-awareness.ca), Project Look Smart (www.ithaca.edu/looksharp), Media Education Foundation (www.mediaed.org), Digital Media Learning Central (www.dmlcentral.net), Classroom 2.0 (www.classroom20.com), Making Curriculum Pop (http://mcpopmb.ning.com), The LAMP (www.thelampnyc.org), and Project New Media Literacies (http://newmedialiteracies.org).

■ *Media watchdogs.* Media watchdogs and critics have much more power to organize counter-propaganda campaigns and boycotts against corporate media. Fox News, for example, is under constant pressure from activist groups that have used the quick dissemination and documentation enabled by the web to launch campaigns against its practices. Broadcast videos can easily be reposted with commentary and fact-checking. Organizations like Media Matters for America (www.mediamatters.org), Free Press (www.freepress.net), and Fairness & Accuracy in Reporting (www.fair.org) are just a few examples of the many watchdogs that take seriously the role of media as a check against the abuse of power. Color of Change (http://colorofchange.org) has successfully targeted bigoted media.

■ *Open systems.* When it comes to computing, some of the most passionate debates surround the difference between *open* and *closed system* software. As mentioned, closed systems like Apple's operating system benefit their users with a safe, crash-proof environment. The danger is that users are dependent on the goodwill of the system controllers. On the other hand, advocates of open operating systems, such as Linux, are far more zealous about the benefits of open software. They argue that despite the dangers of open systems (viruses, spam, crashes, identity theft) their ingrained participatory principle makes them more resilient. Linux, for example, has so many volunteer programmers that it becomes a very robust and well-tested operating system. Open platforms like Google's Android are generative: they enable new possibilities and connections to be made by programmers that don't know each other or may never meet. Open source can be applied to many endeavors: democracy, education, economics, design, architecture, spirituality, etc. The thing that all of these have in common is their participatory nature. However, because they are open systems, it should be noted that all these tools can also be co-opted by corporate powers. For example, flash mobs and culture jamming—examples of open systems media because of their participatory nature—are also used by marketers to cut through the clutter of traditional advertising.

These various strands come together in what Wael Ghonim calls Revolution 2.0. A Google executive and leading figure during the Egyptian uprising that toppled Hosni Mubarak in 2011, Ghonim argues that what happened in Cairo's Tahrir Square is very similar to how Wikipedia works: everyone contributes something small to create and build upon an idea that is much greater than the sum of its parts. The "psychological barrier of fear," he says, was broken down because people found each other through their networks—virtual and physical—in order to collaborate leaderlessly through people-to-people contact. Such is the Jeffersonian ideal in which media help facilitate and enlarge the possibility for human experience rather than limit and control it.

But making the Jeffersonian model a reality requires tremendous vigilance and conscientious practice through activism and the promotion of alternative tools. As biology teaches us, the structure of systems—be they open or closed—organizes relationships and effects. Thus "prefigurative" politics, which means you practice and live the change you want to see in the world, become the mantra of the Jeffersonian ideal.

To say that we can only use open or closed tools is to propose a false choice. In some respects, the planet is in such peril that we need to connect by any means necessary. Should I not go to a demonstration because the only way I can get there is by car, a primary instrument of the world capitalist order? This is not to say that people who refuse technology or withdraw from the system are wrong. Maybe if enough people withdrew their support it would collapse the system. On the other hand, the resilience of the system is that it makes us dependent on its resources to survive. It's very difficult, if not impossible, to live 100 percent free of the world system. I'm a bigger fan of engagement. Through interaction and contact with the system we do what chaos theoreticians argue, making global change on a local level.

Occupy the Media

A good example of the Jeffersonian model in practice has been prototyped by the Occupy movement. New media and cultural practices mirror each other in the same way that contemporary gamers now view the world differently than gamers of old. Consider how baseball evolved with radio. Its slow pace is perfect for the narrative storytelling style of the oral tradition. American football, on the other hand, is perfect for television, its visually impressive and vignette-driven coverage timed perfectly for the commercial break. In both cases, though, their dissemination requires top-down distribution and offers clear and definitive outcomes, making them excellent fodder for discussion, distraction, and catharsis. Not surprisingly, politics have come to mirror sports spectacles with teams (parties) and strategies (platforms) that have a way of eschewing actual discussion of issues, substituting real politics with horse-race-like coverage.

No wonder the native intellectuals of the colonial media system can't deal with the open-ended politics of kids raised on "infinite" games. Infinite games are about keeping the gameplay going, not about definitive winners and losers. The goal of infinite games is not an "end game"—as so many corporate media pundits search for in the narrative of the movement—but sustainability. How do you keep it going? "It," in our case, is not the system designed to benefit the colonists, but life for the rest of us who want to raise our children on a healthy planet and in a prosperous and just society. In zero-sum games the focus on ends has a distinctly Western cultural spin. We are indoctrinated to believe that the struggle between winners and losers is the nature of our world, going as deeply as the Judeo-Christian narrative that underlies the world system. The premature declarations that capitalism had won the Cold War justified American imperial expansion because it was argued that we were finally at the end of history and that global expansion of a U.S.–led world system was inevitable.

But now this narrative is challenged in a big way by an emerging global youth revolution, best exemplified by the Occupy movement and the Arab Spring. According to journalist Paul Mason's extensive research, these planetary youths have several characteristics in common. Not only are they technologically savvy "graduates with no future," they are everywhere. Ironically, these conditions are a by-product of globalization's boom years. Revolution appears to be the flipside of the world system's diffusion around the globe. According to Mason, activist media tactics can be generalized as follows. Facebook (or other social networks) are used to establish groups with "strong but flexible connections." Twitter then becomes a conduit for updates and news that bypass traditional media. Evidence is supplied through YouTube and online photo sharing services like Yfrog, Flickr, and Twitpic. Bloggers create sites that people can link to. The widespread use of mobile phones makes the network immediate and expandable, subverting the hierarchical control maintained by traditional media institutions and expanding the horizon of revolutionary potential.

In the United States the Occupy movement challenged the dominant symbolic order in two different ways. The first was iconic, at the level of memes, and the second was through the actual production tools used to mediate the movement's message. On a symbolic level, Occupiers built on old-school strategies going back to the 1960s, by creating events that mainstream media would inadvertently cover because of their sensational character. In other words, it's possible to "play" the corporate media by turning its economic prerogative for novelty against them.

The Yippies, with the merry prankster Abbie Hoffman at the fore, staged numerous public spectacles to draw attention to the anti-war movement, such as throwing money on the stock exchange floor. Other activists, like artist Joey Skaggs or the Yes Men, use hoaxing as a way for revealing media hypocrisy. Environmental activists like Greenpeace stage media events in order to draw attention to their message. These represent early forms of media occupation because they are strategies for symbolically taking over the dominant discourse without actually controlling the means of production. But what happens when movements like Occupy get absorbed into popular culture? As it turns out, *Law & Order,* the popular TV series filmed in New York City, attempted to incorporate Occupy Wall Street into one of its episodes. When the producers built a replica of Occupy Wall Street's Zucotti Park encampment, the occupiers disrupted the filming and dismantled the simulacra of their spiritual home. But what if MTV made a Real World Occupy Wall Street? Would it mean that corporate media had colonized Occupy, or that Occupy had successfully "occupied" popular culture? I recall once arguing with some younger punks about ideological purity. Nirvana's Kurt Cobain wanted his records to be in Walmart because as a kid in rural, working-class Washington, it was the only way he could be exposed to rock music. The punks, of course, thought this was a terrible example. Nirvana represented the ultimate traitor to indy purity. To the purists I offer the same advice a screenwriter once gave about other writers stealing story concepts: don't act out of jealousy and resentment, just create new ideas.

Some communication theorists argue that problems exist because they are socially constructed. Climate change or economic disparity may be experienced as real world conditions for many people, but until they are defined as problems, they don't exist in terms of public discourse (the way we talk about things). Like the proverbial tree that falls in the forest, we have to hear some noise before issues get aired. The conversation needs to get initiated. So how does this happen? Claim makers have to find ways to get heard or seen. As explained, corporations, as controllers of the major media cartels, dominate public discourse. An example of this is how neoliberal doctrine became a kind of planetary religion. Super slogans with ideologically charged meanings, such as "growth" and "progress," have firmly entrenched connotations that are difficult to dislodge. Challenging this discourse was the primary task of the Occupy movement.

The genius, I think, was the deployment of the simple slogan, "we are the 99 percent." It's like a nuclear missile directed at the global zeitgeist. As a mind bomb it detonates the connections between differing social problems. People get it because they are living it. As a meme it's a flame that ignites, but doesn't necessarily replicate exactly in the same form every time. Like an utterance that echoes and reverberates through resonance, the idea doesn't exist as a thing but as part of an ongoing conversation, a kind of disturbance in the colonial symbolic order. Few need a college degree to apprehend the depth of catastrophe the current economic model has become. By establishing contact zones with the awareness that something needs to be done, these occupations become apertures for an emergent reality that contests the delusional dreamworld propagated by the world system.

Like Scott McCloud's theory of cartooning, concepts with basic outlines and little detail create space for the imagination to explore and fill. This is why a simply drawn Peanuts cartoon appeals to the imagination of little kids, whereas action comic books with greater levels of realism have a tendency to "think" for us. Marshall McLuhan developed a similar concept with his idea of "hot" and "cool" media. Hot media, like film or black-and-white photography, involves fewer senses (such as vision), leaving little for the imagination to explore. Blockbusters, for example, have a way of driving our attention. Experimental films, however, like Terrence Malick's *The Tree of Life,* are cool because of their open-ended narrative structure. Cool media involve more senses and therefore the necessity to fill in the blanks. TV, McLuhan believed, is cool because its multisensory experience requires more interactivity to impose meaning. Its low-definition quality means we are more detached. These concepts are not binary, but a continuum. The main point, returning to the "99 percent" slogan and hashtag character of the Occupy movement, is that it creates space for movement and discussion, a kind of nonlinear interaction that flies in the face of the dominant system's architecture, which is based on reductionism and linear thinking patterns.

The handful of corporate media that dominate the telecommunications environment represent the interests of the "1 percent." The 1 percent media will have difficulty commodifying the reality that people are experiencing on the ground. After all, how long can you get away with calling the opposition hippies, communists, and Nazis and remain credible? This was Frankfurt School researcher Siegfried Kracauer's insight when he studied why Nazi propaganda ultimately failed: it couldn't sustain the contradictions of its own messaging (such as the Nazis were simultaneously invincible yet vulnerable) because it was based entirely on untruths. Kracauer warns that when a propaganda system puts truths and untruths on an equal footing, they cancel each other out. Democracies, he argued, need to tell good stories that have some basis in reality. Unfortunately, the dominant media is not in the reality business. How is it possible that we are simultaneously growing and prospering while real economic and ecological systems collapse? Capitalism can no longer sustain itself by externalizing the crisis, because ultimately there is no such thing as externalization in a planetary community. The financiers might think they can survive by boarding some kind of superliner arks like we saw in the film *2012,* but ultimately food, energy, and labor have to come from somewhere, paid for with real money. Peak oil and peak debt have lead to peak nonsense.

Which brings us to how the Occupy movement self-mediated. The media coming out of the Occupy movement has been as professional, smart, and intelligent as anything made by the colonial media. Already we have seen internet portals, documentaries, newspapers (the Occupied Wall Street Journal, no less), Wikis, Meetup hubs, live streaming, Facebook fan pages, a YouTube channel, Twitter feeds, Tumblr blogs, and photogenic cardboard signs that replicate in the mediasphere. Occupation is reappropriation and recontextualization (add "occupy" label, stir), so it's possible for the Occupied Times of London and Occupied Wall Street Journal to remix titles owned by Rupert Murdoch (Chairman and CEO of News Corp.). All of these have in common an open source approach that incorporates consensus-based working groups, volunteer mediators, and public funding through donations. These media are networked, transparent, collective, and emergent. Most importantly, embedded in their media are ethics based on nonviolence and a monitoring of derogatory speech, such as language that demonizes cops or racially and gendered offensive comments. Additionally, a new breed of movement-inspired documentarians called UpTakers livestreamed Occupy actions utilizing smart phones with special apps. They imposed a kind of uncomfortable transparency on the movement that brought the promoters of violent tactics into conflict with those advancing nonviolence. Advocates of sabotage and violent confrontation prefer their actions remain in the shadows, whereas UpTakers believe in openness, warts and all. Curiously, the disruptive tactics of fringe saboteurs aligns them with police in that both parties want to prevent journalists from documenting their activities. Subsequently, UpTaker media embodies a convergence of the ethical principles I proposed at the beginning of this manifesto by promoting transparent communications that inspire trust, collaboration, reciprocity, and credibility for building healthy communities. It goes without saying that under extreme repression, activists will need to adjust accordingly. But those working in societies that assert freedom and democracy as primary values should challenge the limit of those claims through an open and deep democratic process. And what better way to do that then to engage in ethical media practice.

An example of the different paradigms of Occupy media versus corporate media can be illustrated by the following anecdote. Late in 2011 I became enraptured by Tim Pool's USTREAM live cast of an Occupy Wall Street's action to occupy a vacant lot in Lower Manhattan. When the initial occupation was thwarted by authorities, throughout that evening protestors played cat and mouse with the police as they traversed the city in pursuit of new occupation sites. Pool captured live and uploaded into the planetary net the action as it unfolded. Like the live cast of the Occupiers getting kettled and arrested on the Brooklyn Bridge a few months prior, it was a riveting reprieve from the old, predigested form of media we grew up with. In particular, unlike the canned and predictable action footage one gets on a "reality" program like *Cops,* this footage was unedited and raw without the directives and prerogatives of commercial interests that determine what is "safe" programming.

After dodging the NYPD throughout Manhattan, protestors spontaneously organized a General Assembly in Times Square. Using the people's mic, they "testified" as to why they were part of the Occupation movement, all the while bathed in the surreal glow of corporate media. Times Square is the quintessential spiritual center of the corporate project. Once the seedy underbelly of New York's deviant unconsciousness, since Rudy Giuliani's reign as mayor in the 1990s the open space of 42nd Street has been transformed into a kind of dystopic hydra of capitalist enclosure. A mix of surveillance and marketing über alles, Times Square has become an open air television studio that invites anyone to enter and be mediated by the planetary corporate rulers. A hybrid of advertising and reality TV, there are few other places on Earth where Disneyland, advertising, military, finance, and mass media cohere into a pulsating hum of mediated insanity. And like moths to a flame, people are attracted by the very thing that could ultimately destroy them. To paraphrase Walter Benjamin, not since the Nazis has our own alienation and self-destruction been made to look so beautiful.

Yet as police stood by to protect holiday shoppers and business as usual, a handful of Occupiers bore witness to this insanity (thereby labeled by the system as lunatics). Here, as the embodiment of Earth's spirit, these brave souls momentarily disrupted the pulsating spectacle. Whilst in the past numerous crazies have attempted such sacrilege against this colonizing machine, something has changed.

The message is being heard. And it's resonating.

It's happening despite the luminous power of Times Square and its tentacled financiers in Wall Street. A people's mic, which is a spontaneous form of direct democracy and speech with high instantaneous feedback, utterly contradicts the communication forms of advertising in which psychologically tested and honed messages are pushed into people's mindspace. The occupiers waged guerrilla war against that mechanism through the deployment of prefigurative politics that pulled people together with a shared sense of responsibility and reciprocity. Their collectivity, community, and ritual become an alternate form of mediation that deprives the corporate powers of their ability to colonize human energy. Such moments of autonomous collectivity—which are increasingly more common—are signs that we have reached the limit and end of the old system and we are currently in a transition into a liminal state in which the previous mental models of the past five hundred years are becoming destabilized.

To mark the two-month anniversary of the initial occupation of Zucotti Park, on November 17, 2011, occupiers organized a day of coordinated action in Manhattan. That evening, as protesters marched across the Brooklyn Bridge, an extraordinary event occurred. Like the bat signal launched into Gotham City's skyline, a large round spotlight appeared on the side of the Verizon building inscribed with the symbol, "99%." Soon words appeared: "MIC CHECK! / LOOK AROUND / YOU ARE A PART / OF A GLOBAL UPRISING / WE ARE A CRY / FROM THE HEART / OF THE WORLD / WE ARE UNSTOPPABLE / ANOTHER WORLD IS POSSIBLE / HAPPY BIRTHDAY / #OCCUPY MOVEMENT / OCCUPY WALL STREET / [a list of cities, states, and countries] / OCCUPY EARTH / WE ARE WINNING / IT IS THE BEGINNING OF THE BEGINNING / DO NOT BE AFRAID / LOVE." The projection served as an instant morale booster; not only did it uplift with their feet on the ground struggling day in and day out with various assaults on their movement and bodies, it also quickly spread through the internet. Magazines and newspapers wrote about it. A documentary on how the project was made and its source code were uploaded to the net. That a localized guerrilla media action used one of the world's biggest telecom company headquarters as its canvas and became a global media phenomena utterly shatters the world system's colonial model.

In a sense, we are experiencing a networked version of Martin Luther's protest in 1517. Like the ninety-five theses he posted on the church door, which later was reprinted and widely disseminated with the new media technology of that period—the printing press—we now see an unprecedented diffusion of an alternative paradigm that challenges the power structure through participatory media technology. This 99 percent bat signal serves as a kind of updated thesis. Whereas Luther challenged the corrupt authority and abuse of power by the Roman

Catholic Church, Occupiers the world over do the same against current dogma by contesting the domination and colonization of human experience by corporations. Clear evidence shows that post-Zucotti Park, the economic discourse in the United States has changed significantly. Income inequality, which was once practically taboo, became central to the debate about the direction of society. Even Republican presidential candidates cribbed notes from Occupy. But it will become necessary to move this discussion even further to link economic issues with the environment. The degradation of our biosphere and economic collapse are two sides of the same coin. It is now time to upgrade the global revolution to put climate change on an equal footing with economic injustice.

Media (Re)Occupation

For good reason Native Americans and other oppressed land-based groups like the Palestinians might object to the "occupation" metaphor. Occupation is associated with conquest and colonization. In fact, in response to concerns of Native Americans, one group in New Mexico changed its name to Reoccupy Albuquerque. In reality the contemporary, emerging occupations around the world are really struggles to re-occupy the commons: these efforts are meant to contest and reverse the colonizing privatization of the planet, and hence defend the dignity of our living systems. Consequently, I mean to use the term in the neutral sense, as a way of describing the taking up of a position in relation to the global economic project that will destroy the biosphere, or at least make it immanently uninhabitable, if it is not stopped.

An example of media (re)occupiers can be found in Flagstaff, Arizona. There a group of punk Native Americans developed their own brand of do-it-yourself media activism, combining their sacred perspective of the land with political activism and punk attitude. Billing their project as the Outta Your Backpack Media Collective, they developed a clever portable media production studio that fits nicely into a skateboarder's rucksack. They produce short videos about resisting the dominant system, contesting current mining operations, and protesting the desecration of their sacred mountain. They host film festivals, train youths in media production, and post their work to YouTube. These indigenous decolonists are prototypical media occupiers, reappropriating the tools of the oppressive system to tell new stories and to network with other youth media makers and storytellers from around the world. By hybridizing their indigenous cultural heritage with media technology, these innovative youth bridge the ancient past with the emerging future.

Such practices fall under the ethical framework for green media citizenship that I have outlined through this manifesto. Further refining the project of green cultural citizenship, the following can be incorporated into thinking about how to democratize and green media:

■ *Disrupt the symbolic order.* Symbols are tied to power and discourse. Use whatever means necessary to break the world system's disastrous monologue through billboard liberation, culture jamming, pranking, guerrilla theater, flash mobs, Temporary Autonomous Zones, etc.

■ *Be tactical, not strategic.* Strategies are for battlefields and sports. Your mind is not Monday Night Football. Be tactical by selectively disrupting colonial rule; be subversive where it counts.

■ *Community is not a demographic.* Don't sell out your communities to commercial interests. Resist commodification by acting like a human and not a list of interests.

■ *Stop glamorizing.* Media's biggest hook is ego gratification. Take seriously the indigenous belief that cameras steal souls.

■ *Produce more media than you consume.* Create new forms of communication and participate.

■ *Strategically use copyright and creative commons.* Share with the world your art and culture, but protect it from colonization. Use appropriate measures to ensure it is protected, but also keep it sharable.

■ *Act globally, think locally.* Learn to think within your landscape. Relocalize consciousness, ground it into Earth and your bioregion. Become a node in the global movement, but don't think like other people. Respect and celebrate your unique cultural identity while honoring global ethics.

- *Think ecologically.* The economics of media systems is based on energy consumption. Use ecology as a reference point to learn how it works.

- *Create media gardens.* Don't just hang out in Twitter and Facebook. Hang out with friends, family, and neighbors by relocating media to the place you live. Host film festivals, house concerts, reading groups, poetry slams, music festivals, jam sessions. Gather and celebrate life. Corporations will come and go, but art, poetry, and music remain.

- *Keep communication systems open.* Choose open operating systems, advocate for equal access to the net, and restrict corporate media monopolies.

- *Push for green technology and labor justice.* Our gadgets and their energy consumption are choking the planet and killing the people who make and dispose of them. Fight for better design and laws that protect workers and the environment.

- *Make communication sacred.* The dominant model of media is to make communication an instrument of commerce. Sacred media starts with the principle that all communication is sacred: it is embedded within our spiritual being. Words start with our breath. What we communicate is intention and a spiritual attitude that becomes a spell cast upon the world. Don't feed the trolls.

- *Know your mind.* Through mindfulness become aware of how your attention is hooked. Learn and understand the methods of manipulation and control that cause you to give away your power.

- *Know your relations.* Mindfully engage the relations you cultivate through the media. Build strong and meaningful relationships, and bridge your participation with your personal life. Are you behaving like a demographic, or are you an active member of your community? Enter into open relations; stop the enclosure of the commons.

- *Know your environment.* No matter where you are, there you are. Be aware of the environments that engage your attention. What do these environments (be they computer interfaces, shopping malls, churches, or forests) demand of your awareness? What possibilities or restrictions do they afford?

- *Know your gadget.* Our media gadgets are part of vast networks of material extraction, production, and waste. They are also programmed to do some things and not others. Disengage those systems of power that are enabling environmental destruction and injustice.

- *Know your connectivity.* Every screen is a portal. Such portals are nodes into vast possibilities of experience. Enter into these space/places ("splaces") with eyes wide open and feet on the ground.

Bringing the world back into balance means that decolonial media must also be implicitly green. The democratization of media shouldn't just be anthropocentric, but ecocentric. The challenge is to become aware of how our media practice is colonized and colonizes the lifeworld.

The Beginning Is Near

Italian piazzas are designed to be no larger than the distance it takes to recognize somebody from afar. Likewise, Greeks believed democratic participation should extend no further than a day's walk from one end of a population center to the other. Such notions of proximity as a key ingredient for civic participation have been crippled by car culture and television. Yet we are also on the cusp of a great global movement that repurposes these ancient notions of local engagement, but the key difference is our ability to now network and connect over vast distances. Thus it was possible in 2003 for up to thirty million people around the world to mobilize regional protests against the impending Iraq War. This is globalization on a different scale imagined by the world system, what the *New York Times* called "the other superpower." By coordinating actions that spanned a twenty-four hour period around the globe, the peace movement glocalized: pressuring local authorities while sending a message to the planetary rulers. Although the invasion wasn't stopped, to borrow from an old military cliché, that particular battle was lost, but not necessarily the war for peace. In hindsight we had the moral authority and were right about the consequences of that illegal war. This time the coming planetary Occupation will not fail: 2003 was a dress rehearsal for something much bigger.

In 2003, for the most part the media cartels downplayed or outright ignored the historical significance of that planetary protest event. They were still enraptured by the spell of 9/11, which gave the United State's military and political rulers carte blanche to invade and destroy any country they pleased. Eventually the media turned on Bush, mainly because of the lesson about Nazi propaganda: no lies can ultimately shield what is actually happening on the ground. Eventually reality bites back. The failure of the wars, political systems, economies, and ecosystems are doing just that. The combination of these undeniable crises and people glocalizing their response through Occupations has made it impossible for the corporate media to ignore the truths that resonate with the greater population.

But getting media coverage is a small part of the strategy. It certainly helps to get the message out to isolated populations: the fact that it is done by people getting together in public spaces with handwritten cardboard signs makes the irony that much greater. Good old-fashioned civic politics draws on our ancient, democratic traditions. The slow, deliberate consensus process taking place during Occupy General Assemblies with their cumbersome people's mic has managed to capture—*occupy*—the public imagination. These practices are not necessarily new—anyone who has done activist work over the years will recognize the form. In the past we did it in the absence of media interest, so for the majority of people, these activities didn't exist. That it now magnetizes vast numbers of people despite a vast propaganda network shows the innate power of awakened consciousness.

The various occupations taking place around the world are connected to ancient cultural practices of communion and ritual. The difference is that the modern technological infrastructure enables local reclamations of the commons to network on a planetary scale. Youth movements around the world, as is the case with the Arab Spring of 2011, *indignatos* in the Mediterranean, or Occupy, significantly inspire and impact the global symbolic order. To put this in terms of Joseph Campbell's concept of the hero's journey, the global disorder created by capitalism is in the process of being restored to balance. As such, people deploy new symbolic relations, be it the Earth photo from space popularized by the environmental movement, the Guy Fawkes mask from *V for Vendetta* repurposed by the Anonymous hacker underground and Occupiers across the globe, or *Avatar*'s memes. These movements find solidarity through symbolic resonances made in the planetary cultural commons. As such, the spirit of DIY at the core of this emerging media occupation has a lineage to not just punk, but hip hop, Situationists, hippies, Dadaists, anticolonists, indigenous resistance, ecological activists, and decentralized global justice movements across the world. We have a great heritage of radical critique and action to build upon, a history that gets relearned with every new generation. As one popular meme to emerge from the Occupy movement states, the beginning is near. By greening our media ecosystems with ecological intelligence, we combine the figurative circle and cross to become resilient in the face of tremendous upheaval and change.

Because of our active participation and engagement, the media ecosystem is coming alive. Its conscious evolution is now in our hands. Like media gardeners prepping the soil, it's time to get our hands dirty.

Author's Note

This book is dedicated to my grandmother, Beatrice López Vigil (1912–2011), who embodied the wisdom of the cultural commons. She lived a full and vigorous life, serving as a great teacher to all those who came into contact with her.

To preserve the tone and immediacy of a manifesto, a bibliography has been omitted from this text. However, out of respect to all my intellectual and spiritual ancestors whose shoulders I lurch upon, and in order to further link beyond this text, a website with a section-by-section bibliography has been created (www.themediaecosystem.com). Likewise, readers who wish to share additional examples not cited in the text can post them to the book's website. Some portions and snippets in this book previously appeared in essays for Reality Sandwich and my blog, http://mediacology.com. The section on hip hop is based on an essay I co-authored with Mike Ipiotis, "The Fifth Element of Hip Hop."

My personal thanks for bringing this book into existence extends first to Daniel Pinchbeck, who prompted me to write it. I also want to recognize the folks at Reality Sandwich, in particular Ken Jordan and Jonathan Philips, for giving me a space to rant about media. I also wish to extend my gratitude to the staff at North Atlantic Books for their kind and gentle handling of a complex manuscript. Doug Reil, Erin Wiegand, and Denise Silva are saints! Also, thanks to my sister, Nicola López, for generously offering one of her fine works of art for the cover design.

I'm indebted to Chet Bowers for inspiring me with the idea of the cultural commons. I also want to express appreciation for Chellis Glendinning who opened my eyes to the world of ecopsychology. Thanks to Randy Hayes who helped me recall the details of Thomas Banyacya's Hopi story. And of course, my blessings and gratitude to the surviving members of the Banyacya clan for dealing with us *bahana*. I'm also thankful for inspiration and ideas from my PhD cohort and mentors at Prescott College. Likewise, a shout out to my homies at NYC's Dharma Punx sangha whose 'tude and sagacity permeate the book. Peace out to the planetary occupiers. Your bravery is an inspiration! Most importantly, gratitude to my family—Cristina, Kika, and Yasmin—for putting up with the mood swings, mental derangement, exhaustion, and stress that accompany the writing process.

Finally, deep appreciation for Gaia, who ultimately called upon me to do this work and to serve. Mitakuye Oyasin.

Antonio López is a media educator and journalist who has written for *Tricycle, Punk Planet, In These Times, High Times, The Brooklyn Rail,* Reality Sandwich, and scores of other magazines, newspapers, websites, and academic journals. His essays have been featured in several anthologies, including *Toward 2012: Perspectives on the Next Age* and the MacArthur Foundation's book series, *Digital Learning in the 21st Century.* His first book on media and education, *Mediacology,* was published in 2008. López received professional training at the Center for Investigative Reporting in San Francisco and studied peace and conflict studies at University of California, Berkeley. He received an MA in media studies from the New School for Social Research and holds a PhD from the School of Punk Rock. He currently resides in Rome, Italy, where he teaches media studies at an American university and is completing his PhD in education for sustainability. He blogs at http://mediacology.com.

EVOLVER EDITIONS promotes a new counterculture that recognizes humanity's visionary potential and takes tangible, pragmatic steps to realize it. EVOLVER EDITIONS explores the dynamics of personal, collective, and global change from a wide range of perspectives.

EVOLVER EDITIONS is an imprint of the nonprofit publishing house North Atlantic Books and is produced in collaboration with Evolver LLC, a company founded in 2007 that publishes the web magazine Reality Sandwich (www .realitysandwich.com), runs the social network Evolver.net (www.evolver.net), and recently launched a new series of live video seminars, Evolver Intensives (www.evolverintensives.com). Evolver also supports the Evolver Social Movement, which is building a global network of communities who collaborate, share knowledge, and engage in transformative practices.

For more information: please visit
www.evolvereditions.com.